I AM @ WORK

Unleashing the Power of Divine Self on the Job!

KELLI JAREAUX

Copyright © 2020 by Kelli Jareaux ISBN 978-1-7338705-2-8

All rights reserved. No part of this publication may be reproduced, stored in or introduced into a retrieval system, distributed, or transmitted in any form or by any means, including photocopying, recording, or other electronic or mechanical methods, without the prior written permission of the publisher, except in the case of brief quotations embodied in critical reviews and certain other noncommercial uses permitted by copyright law. For permission requests, write to the publisher, addressed "Attention: Permissions Coordinator," at the address below.

GROW Publishing: info@GROWContinuum.com

Ordering Information: info@GROWContinuum.com

Quantity sales: Special discounts are available on quantity purchases by corporations, associations, and others. For details, contact the publisher at the address above.

Orders by U.S. trade bookstores and wholesalers. Please contact GROW Publishing Distribution: Contact info@GROWContinuum.com.

Events, locales, and conversations have been recreated from the author's memory, and in some instances, stories have been fictionalized to emphasize a point or to maintain anonymity. Also, to maintain their anonymity, in some instances the author has changed the names of individuals, businesses, and places, and changed or embellished some identifying circumstances, characteristics, and details, such as physical properties, occupations, and places of residence.

This book is for informational purposes. The author and publisher do not assume and hereby disclaim any liability to any party for any loss, damage, or disruption caused by information provided herein, whether through its use, misuse, defect, inaccuracy, accuracy, or for any other reason. The author and publisher make no guarantees, warranties, or promises concerning the effects or outcomes a reader may experience as a result of applying the techniques, suggestions, tips, ideas, processes, or strategies contained herein. This book is not a substitute for professional advice, counseling, or coaching.

Consult a professional, especially in matters relating to mental health and any symptoms that may require diagnosis or medical attention. Although the author and publisher have made every effort to ensure that the information in this book was correct at press time, the author and publisher disclaim any liability to any party for errors or omissions, whether such errors or omissions result from negligence, accident, or any other cause.

Printed in the United States of America. All rights reserved under International Copyright Law. Contents and/or cover may not be reproduced in whole or in part in any form without the express written consent of the Publisher.

This book includes the limited and fair use of Scriptures, Sacred Text, and other information for educational purposes. Where appropriate the author has attributed information to its source in the endnotes.

For my mother, Phyllis Crummer, whose loving reminders kept me from forgetting that my life is the story God has entrusted me with and my work is to tell it.

For my father, Rowland "Pat" Crummer, my hero, always!

For my sister, Leslie Williams, a dazzling light in whose shadow I would have remained had she not always been my biggest cheerleader.

And, for my son and sweetest love, Kaleb Jareaux, who is a perfect example of what it means to be yourself always in all ways!

You are my heart!

Acknowledgments

In all of Your many forms, by all of Your names, and in all of Your embodiments, Thank You, God! Thank You for my grandmother, Lola B. Crummer, whose rocking chair and Bible were fixtures in my life. Thank You for the spiritual dedication demonstrated by my aunt, May Elizabeth Means. Thank You for the example and teachings of my "aunt" Roxy Schumann. Thank You for the love of a family that is always perfect. Thank You for the GROW Continuum and my Co-Pastor, angel, and constant support, Reverend Angela Whitmal. Thank You for the incredible love, teachings, and support of my IVISD Family, especially my editor, Reverend Beverly Biddle, and book contributor, Reverend Candas Ifama Barnes, Founder Reverend Doctor Iyanla Vanzant, and Mama Almasi Wilcots, Mama Helen Jones, Mama Muhsinah Berry-Dawan and all of the Mamas, here and beyond. Thank You for all of the Spirituality-At-Work Champions, whose stories are included in this book. Thank You for the support and teachings of the Etherean Mission, Brother Ishmael Tetteh, and Reverend Doreene Hamilton. Thank You for the assistance of Author Larry Chang. Thank You for Richelle Hill and the entire Hill Family, my second family. Thank You for my first self-chosen spiritual home, Unity of Washington, DC, and Reverend Sylvia Sumpter. Thank You for Beverly Douglas and her aunt, the late Mary Hall. Thank You for Master Coach Ron Davis, who taught me it is safe to express all of who I am in Spirit! And thank You for all who have loved me and supported my spiritual growth, the many unnamed beloved ones, who have touched me and grew me in ways known and unknown.

Note about how the book was created.

Dear Beloved Friend,

Thank you for claiming your copy of I AM @ Work: Unleashing the Power of Divine Self on the Job!

This book will teach you critical skills, tools, techniques, and more for unleashing your Divine Self at work. This is information every person who wants to experience God on the job needs to understand and apply.

Much of the content in the book was created during a live interview. For this reason, it reads like a conversation rather than a traditional book that talks *at* you.

I wanted you to feel as though I am talking *with* you, much like a close friend or relative. Though I added to the information discussed in the interview, I maintained the interview format as a literary device.[1]

I felt that creating the material this way would make it easier to grasp the topics and put them to use quickly.

So . . . relax.

Grab a pen or pencil and some paper to take notes.

Get ready to take your experience of spirituality at work to the next level. Prepare yourself to discover your True Work and how to advance that work, regardless of your job!

Let us get started with integrating spirituality into your life on the job for a better world and more work satisfaction and success right now.

Lovingly yours,

Reverend Kelli

Table of Contents

Introduction	1
Book I: NOW	13
Chapter 1	15
Declare Your Authority	
Chapter 2	31
Invite God to Your Job	
Chapter 3	39
Do not Believe the Hype:	
Your Job Is Not Your True Work	
Chapter 4	49
Worthy Work: Knowing the	
Divine Value of What You Do	
Chapter 5	59
Fearless Office Politics for Spiritual Pros	
Chapter 6	67
Activate the Ultimate Work Mindset	
Chapter 7	77
If You Build It, God WILL Come:	
Building Your Spiritual Toolkit	
Chapter 8	101
Design Your Time: The Zen of Where and When	
Chapter 9	109
Free Yourself from the Groupthink Trap!	

Chapter 10   129
*Walk the Sacred Path of the
Spirituality-at-Work Champion*

Chapter 11   157
*Stop Dying to Make a Living:
Choose Divinity, Not Karoshi*

Book II: THEN   167

101 Simple Coaching Tips to Ascend Beyond Challenges in Your Workplace   169

    Tip No. 1   171
    Be Kind to All Always.

    Tip No. 2   172
    Have a Good Handshake.

    Tip No. 3   173
    Be Careful with Credit Cards.

    Tip No. 4   174
    Use the Magic Formula.

    Tip No. 5   176
    Be an Effective Timekeeper.

    Tip No. 6   177
    *Do Not Send
    Organization-wide Emails.*

    Tip No. 7   179
    Limit Personal Phone Calls.

    Tip No. 8   180
    *Keep Your Side Business
    Your Business.*

    Tip No. 9   181
    Do Not Bring Your Kids to Work.

Tip No. 10
Be Punctual. — 183

Tip No. 11
No Shouting. — 184

Tip No. 12
No Crying. — 185

Tip No. 13
No Scolding. — 186

Tip No. 14
No Blaming. — 187

Tip No. 15
No Petting. — 188

Tip No. 16
No Excessive Surfing. — 189

Tip No. 17
No Elicit Emailing. — 190

Tip No. 18
Do Not Do Any Work, Send Any Emails, or Store Any Documents that Can Get You Fired If Discovered. — 191

Tip No. 19
Do Not Gossip. — 192

Tip No. 20
Choose Carefully When Involving Yourself with Peers. — 193

Tip No. 21
Identify and Remain Loyal to a Mentor. — 194

Tip No. 22
Protect Your Bosses and Be Publicly Loyal to Them. — 195

Tip No. 23
Criticism Often Backfires. 196

Tip No. 24
Publicly Maintain a Positive Attitude. 197

Tip No. 25
Be Eager. 198

Tip No. 26
Let It Be Widely Known that You Love What You Do. 199

Tip No. 27
Be Confident, But Not Overconfident. 200

Tip No. 28
Be Truthful. 201

Tip No. 29
Be Diplomatic. 202

Tip No. 30
Be Direct. 203

Tip No. 31
Be Well-Liked by Opponents. 204

Tip No. 32
Leave Your Personal Life at Home, Verbally, and Attitudinally. 205

Tip No. 33
Acknowledge Personal Crises that Directly Impact Your Work Performance. 206

Tip No. 34
No Sexism. No Racism. No Homophobia. 207

Tip No. 35
Do Not Deride or Defend Peers. 208

Tip No. 36
Do Not Cut Corners.   209

Tip No. 37
*Business Casual Does
Not Mean Business Bum.*   210

Tip No. 38
*Do Not Date or Sleep with Anyone
Employed by the Company.*   211

Tip No. 39
Get Involved.   212

Tip No. 40
Be Polite.   213

Tip No. 41
Watch Your Body Language.   214

Tip No. 42
Pay Attention to Advice.   215

Tip No. 43
Create New Work for Yourself.   216

Tip No. 44
Request Training.   217

Tip No. 45
*Use Care When Involving
Yourself in Pro-Bono
or Charitable Projects.*   218

Tip No. 46
*Do Not Get a Reputation
for Socializing.*   219

Tip No. 47
Evaluate Subordinates Honestly.   220

Tip No. 48 221
Get Clients.

Tip No. 49 222
*Know Trends in the Area of Your
Specialization and News and
Current Events, But Do Not
Be Overly Opinionated.*

Tip No. 50 223
Have a Sense of Humor!

Tip No. 51 224
*Exhibit Your Best Personality,
Not Your Worst.*

Tip No. 52 225
*Come to the Table with a
Plan or Suggestion.*

Tip No. 53 226
Follow Through.

Tip No. 54 227
*Beware: Publicly Challenging a
Colleague, Co-Worker or Boss Is
an Invitation to Open Conflict.*

Tip No. 55 228
Do Not Pilfer Supplies.

Tip No. 56 229
Know that What You Say Will Travel.

Tip No. 57 230
*Purchase a Home, a Car, or
Whatever Else Makes Sense for
You. But, Do Not Overextend.*

Tip No. 58 231
*Do Not Hide, Tell
Them Who You Are.*

Tip No. 59 232
*Expect to Bear the Burden
of Miscommunications.*

Tip No. 60 233
*To Gain New Recruits or Clients Your
Firm or Company May Attempt to Use
Your Status as a Minority or Any Other
Status You Hold.*

Tip No. 61 235
Check-in.

Tip No. 62 236
Do Not Get Lost.

Tip No. 63 237
Delegate, as Necessary.

Tip No. 64 238
Get Familiar.

Tip – 239
Make Friends with Support People.

Tip No. 66 240
Be Independent.

Tip No. 67 242
Have Facetime!

Tip No. 68 243
*Have Enough Work to Be Able
to Come in on the Weekend.*

Tip No. 69 244
Do Not Be Intimidated by Bosses.

Tip No. 70 245
*Do Not Be Intimidated by
the Ambition of Others.*

Tip No. 71
Be Thoughtful.   **246**

Tip No. 72
Do Not Be Silent.   **247**

Tip No. 73
Confront But Do Not Be Confrontational.   **248**

Tip No. 74
Do Keep Options Open But Do Not Be Indiscreet in Seeking Other Employment.   **250**

Tip No. 75
Pick a Mentor in the Middle, Not Too Big or Too Small a Fish.   **251**

Tip No. 76
Ask Open-Ended Questions.   **252**

Tip No. 77
Ask "How Did You?" Questions. "If You Were Me, How Would You?" Questions. "What Would You Suggest?" Questions.   **253**

Tip No. 78
Be Switzerland. Stay Neutral.   **254**

Tip No. 79
Do Not Be Baited.   **255**

Tip No. 80
Do Not Be Obvious in Circumventing the Chain of Command or Whistleblowing.   **256**

Tip No. 81
Do Show Interest and Volunteer for Work on Issues that Interest You.   **257**

Tip No. 82 — 258
Keep Your Boss Informed.

Tip No. 83 — 259
Spend Quality Time with Family.

Tip No. 84 — 260
Check How You Are Progressing.

Tip No. 85 — 261
*Stand for Yourself from
the Very Beginning!*

Tip No. 86 — 262
Negotiate Outcomes that You Desire.

Tip No. 87 — 263
Do Not Brown-nose.

Tip No. 88 — 264
*Do Not Step on Toes
or Put Down Ideas.*

Tip No. 89 — 265
Answer Questions to the Third Tier.

Tip No. 90 — 267
Specify the Parameters of Your Work.

Tip No. 91 — 268
Be a Good Boss to Those You Oversee.

Tip No. 92 — 269
Give Credit Where It Is Due.

Tip No. 93 — 270
Do Not Be Thin-Skinned.

Tip No. 94 — 271
Do Not Make Rushed Judgments.

Tip No. 95
*Make Your "Yes" Mean "Yes,"
and Your "No" Mean "No."*   272

Tip No. 96
Offer Support.   273

Tip No. 97
Show Much Appreciation!   274

Tip No. 98
Pick Your Battles Carefully.   275

Tip No. 99
Befriend Lame Ducks.   276

Tip No. 100
Never Rest on Your Laurels.   277

Tip No. 101
*Do Not Rely on Promises.
Be Your Own Leverage.*   278

Conclusion   279

Index   287

Endnotes   291

Introduction

Wherever you are, that is your platform, your stage, your circle of influence. That is your talk show, and that is where your power lies.

~ Oprah Winfrey ~

I Am @ Work has been culled from my own cathartic journey through work into Divine Identity. This book and my expertise concerning how to unleash Divinity on the job are both products of my own experiences with God on the job. Using the techniques discussed here, God, through Divine alignment, transformed me.

Like so many other Americans, I had misinterpreted the dream.

Once upon a time, I allowed my job to shape the direction of my growth. Instead of falling in love with my Divine Self, I became a creation of my employer. And I resented my inauthentic, corporate self. My resentment was offset by the stature, external affirmations, and admiration that I received from others, especially when I sported the latest, greatest exterior symbol of success. Still, it did not take long to feel burdened by the person I had become—a person with an ego I constantly had to feed with more stuff, for more applause, from more people. It was a bottomless pit, an exhausting cycle of emptiness. I had acquired the accouterments of the American Dream, but I was starved for something I did not have and could not buy. I felt sad and betrayed, hoodwinked, and bamboozled. I felt the promise of the dream itself was a lie.

In retrospect, I understand that like so many other Americans, I had misinterpreted the dream.

I believed it was about achieving financial independence through hard work, spending, living lavishly, and displaying my success. Now, I understand that as metal becomes a magnet by touching a magnet, for me the dream is about regularly touching my own depths, the place where I unite with Spirit, and through that touching, becoming more of what God is seeking to be through me. I see a job as the staging area for my True Work. It focuses my mind and drives me to gather and focus my energy.

My first real job sparked within me a fire for solving things. My mind would constantly cycle back to the challenges my cases posed, particularly if I had developed a personal relationship with the client. Though my obsession often meant I was not fully present with my family and friends, with the details of my life, or with thoughts of God, still work enthralled me. Like the unceasing prayer described by Paul, in 1 Thessalonians 5:17, my mind was unceasingly occupied with doing the work of weaving unwinnable facts into winning arguments and strategizing ways to push and pull people into deals that would be considered a win for me and my client. This was immensely pleasurable. It was intellectual cocaine. And it was the Hand of Spirit pointing in the direction of my True Work: creative problem-solving.

Regardless of the horror show that your job may be, always remember it is a fertile opportunity. It provides you with 30, 40, or more hours per week to contact the tranquility of your soul, to focus your mind, to gather and direct your energies, and to discover what God is seeking to do through you.

Getting Your House in Order

As you explore the journey to integrate spiritual practices into your life on the job, I encourage you to reflect on your overall experience of Spirit. How do you experience your spiritual connection? Is it as powerful as you want it to be when you are away from work, or is work just the place where its absence is most noticeable? My goal in life—a goal I recommend to you—is to be Divine Self everywhere.

> Be Divine Self everywhere.

To do this, you will need to know how to push your own buttons, how to activate your own experience of God wherever and whenever you desire, and with as much ease and as little effort as possible.

My jobs have evolved into a refuge for me. As a contractor for many different employers on many different matters, I am less prone to yield to emotional or ego-driven desires. I am more likely to align with Spirit now than before when I was attempting to climb the ladder to partnership. Home is tougher. At home, my identity has a continuity that people are invested in. They want me to be the same. They want me to follow customs or their dictates. I am emotionally invested in them. The tentacles of our attachment to one another are interwoven tightly. At home, the stakes are high! There are more distractions, and so many other things to focus on besides strengthening my connection and feeling in communion with God.

> The strategies you develop and apply at work also will support the development of your at-home practice.

If you have already mastered your home practice, congratulations! In my opinion, you have done the hard part. I will show you how to make experiencing God on the job the easy part.

If you have not yet mastered an at-home spiritual practice, do not worry. There is no defined order to the process of spiritual growth. The strategies you develop and apply at work also will support the development of your at-home practice.

I do want to alert you to three issues that typically begin at home and then bleed into and disrupt your performance on the job: (1) un-forgiveness, (2) dysfunctional family of origin or significant other issues, and (3) betrayal. I recommend that you explore whether these issues impact you. If so, you can use the tools in this book to resolve them so that they do not wreak havoc on the job.

What is in a Name?

I was very intentional in naming this book. Genesis 2:19-20 tells us that God gave Adam naming power. We also have the power to name.[2] And, the power to name a thing is the power to define it, and the power to Divine it. Naming is co-creating in that it creates a mold or a template for the Divine to fulfill. It has been said that a name is a self-fulfilling prophecy. Naming announces to the universe what you desire the thing to be and what you want it to become. I named this book, *I AM @ Work* because I desired it to be a portal that transports readers through the continuum from the individual "I am" to the Divine "I AM," from the individual at work, to God, Spirit, the Divine at work. Here, the term *work* refers not only to the place that employs or the place where work is done but also to the work itself. Work is the act of becoming, the process of being. It is the action of the Divine out-picturing or manifesting itself, making its presence known.

> *The very act of being you is a form of doing your work.*

We are always at work. In one sense, work happens every time we interact with and impact the world. In other words, the very act of being you is a form of doing your work.

The Bible in John 5:17 quotes Jesus speaking on work. He said, "My Father works unceasingly, and so do I." Similarly, in John 9:4, He said in part, "I must work the works of him that sent me . . .." The Weymouth New Testament version of John 9:4 replaces the "I" with "We." It says, "We must do the works of Him who sent me . . .." In another reference, John 14:10 Jesus says, "The words that I speak unto you I speak not of myself: but the Father that dwelleth in me, he doeth the works." The Weymouth New Testament edition puts it this way, "The things that I tell you all I do not speak on my own authority: but the Father dwelling within me carries on His own work."[3]

There is an authority dwelling within each of us. That authority, which I call God, seeks to drive your life at work and home. It seeks to reveal who you truly are, not who you have allowed life to make you. Surrendering to this authority will ease the pressure and stress you feel at home, at work, and in your relationships, even your relationship with yourself. This book will encourage you to stop resisting God, and free yourself to be your Self.

In this book, I have included references to Scripture and Sacred Text, and this is a good time to tell you my views on such things, and, religion and spirituality in general. I love the God I know through my spiritual and religious practices and my life experiences. My intimate relationship with and understanding of God is my own. It is a loving, growing, unrestricted and free relationship. It is not bound by other people's religions or rules. It requires no explaining or defending. It is mine, for me, designed to grow the God Identity that is my destiny.

Because it is not my goal to have you adopt or embrace my religion or even my spiritual practices, you will find in this book techniques and processes to support you in determining what is effective for you, within your own paradigm of religious and spiritual practices and beliefs. My goal is to give you access to a deeper experience of the God of your understanding, the Divine Spirit that indwells you, the Spirit that I believe seeks to express as you, through you, and through your work.

> *The purpose of all things is to draw closer, nearer, and deeper into Divine Identity.*

For me, Scripture or Sacred Text frequently is an entry point. One way I connect with Spirit is through my mind. The words of Scripture arouse the energy of God in me. When that energy is aroused, I can see my true face and experience the essence of my Divine Self. The text is a tool. The text itself is a portal of sorts that aids me in ushering in an identity. It is not the truth or accuracy of the text that matters but the connection the text creates between me and ME, or if you prefer this language, between me and GOD. The text is kindling, but the fire is what matters. Use whatever kindling gets you to the fire. I do. The purpose of all things is to draw closer, nearer, and deeper into Divine Identity.

So, if the use of the Scripture or Sacred Text I have chosen, the mention of smudging or Spirit, or anything else put forth here becomes a barrier or burden, simply release it. The goal is for you to create for yourself a transparent, clear, frictionless connection to who God is becoming as you.

Your presence here on earth is intentional. When God elected to manifest itself in a form named you, God had a plan, an intention to be a certain way and to do certain things. Little space exists between being and doing. It is like the space between water and ice, two expressions of the same energy. I believe our mission is to purify and cleanse ourselves gradually (and sometimes abruptly) shedding our allegiance to the external and delivering this true version of ourselves into the world through our lives and our work. This book is intended to show you how, and to encourage you to commit to bringing that Self forward in your work, at your job, and in all that you do.

The "I AM" of It

In Exodus 3:14, Moses encounters God and asks what God's name is, God replies with an answer that roughly means, I am that I am. Moses sought to name the authority of God, and God responded with, "I am that I am." In Hebrew, "I am" also means "I was" and "I will be." Then later in the New Testament, Jesus is quoted in John 8:58 as having said, "Truly, truly, I say to you, before Abraham was, I am." When they heard his I AM declaration the crowd

God is here, and where God is, all is possible; all is doable, all is already done at the highest possible level.

concluded Jesus was likening himself to God, assuming the title and Divine Identity and authority of God, and thereby blaspheming, so they took up stones to kill him. Throughout the Book of John, Jesus repeatedly uses the I AM authority to align, empower and announce himself, anointing himself the Bread of Life (John 6:35, 41, 48, 51), the Light of the World (John 8:12), the Door of the Sheep (John 10:7, 9), the Good Shepherd (John 10:11, 14), the Resurrection and the Life (John 11:25), the Way, the Truth and the Life (John 14:6), and the True Vine (John 15:1, 5).

> The I AM power is a tipping point.

For me, *I AM* is metaphysical. It is mystical. It is the creative aspect of the Higher Self. It is the God Self and God Itself. It is the battle cry that activates the power and authority of God. It means God is present with me now. God is here, and where God is, all is possible; all is doable, all is already done at the highest possible level.

I began this book's title with *I AM* so that from the very beginning, it would already be done. The God in you who also lives in me already has secured the outcome. So, relax! Sit back! Allow His will to be done in your life, in your work, and at your job.

Unleashing

What happens when an unstoppable force collides with an unmovable object? It depends on where the *I AM* power resides! The I AM power is a tipping point.

For most of us, it is a dormant power that we activate unknowingly and rarely, but we still recognize it. I suspect that you feel the correctness of what I am saying here. I believe you have been called to this book because it is a jumping-off point for the next step in your spiritual evolution. I believe you are no stranger to the miracles of God, and that on some level, you accept yourself as qualified to participate in and even facilitate these miracles. Do not shy away from that! Do not be embarrassed or hide from others the degree of confidence you have in yourself. Your confidence pales in comparison to the level of confidence God has in you!

By reading this book, you are making the request, accepting the assignment, and positioning yourself to shed the false and to reveal the truth. As I sit alone in my living room and write this book, I know I am not alone. This God in us is with me, keeping me aligned, infusing my words with power, ensuring the truth of my promises—Its promises. I know It knows what is needed to unleash the Divine Self of every reader who has been chosen to read this book. I know you have been selected by God to do the work you have come to do. I know because you are reading this book that it is foreordained to support you. Know that for yourself. Stand in this truth no matter what events occur. You are here to do a great work! I am here to aid you in unleashing your Divine power so that you may do that work. This is our shared destiny! I am humbled by it. And, already, I am in awe of you!

The Power of the Divine Self

Many are willing to acknowledge an external God. Fewer are willing to acknowledge the God within. Fewer still are willing to acknowledge God within others. A minuscule number are willing to believe they can unite with and express themselves as God. If you are among those who find this idea unbelievable, no worries! To experience it is to believe it. To do it is to know it. I do not live in a twenty-four-hour state of conscious union with the Divine, and I am not aware of anyone who claims to. But, as the saying goes, shoot for the moon and even if you fail, you will end up among the stars!

My goal in writing this book is to support you in creating a practice. I want you to have a practice that regularly and consistently allows you to recognize and experience the power of your Divine Self. I want you to have a practice that builds your ability to trust in and surrender to your Divine Self, and to activate and unleash it in support of your True Work, whether you are doing that True Work on your job or somewhere else.

On the Job

In this book, you will notice that I use the words, "God" and "Spirit," interchangeably, and also use the phrase, "Divine Self" to refer to your own God Nature or Higher Self. However, when I discuss "work," I distinguish

Your job is a sacred place.

it from the place where work is performed, your "job." Finally, pay attention to the distinction between work and True Work. Most often here, the word "work" refers to your True Work, but in a few cases, it refers to the activity you do at your job or the practice of doing your spiritual work. Where I am referring to your True Work, I will use the phrase "True Work" or capitalize the "W" in "work." In general, you will be clear if you allow context to be your guide. Your job is a sacred place.

It is a field for growing toward your Divine Self. It is a place where priorities are revealed, and choices are made. Your job will rub against you, like a shoe that is too tight. The friction it causes reflects the places where you are misaligned. The job rubs, it whispers, it nudges, then pushes and pulls and screams. It whittles away at the false to reveal the exact need of your soul. Only your True Work will fulfill that need. The discomfort you feel at your job is the universe calling upon you to release the false and to embrace the true. This is the calling. The more you surrender to your calling, the more of your Divine Self you will become, and the more of your True Work you will attract.

> *This book is an ignition switch, intended to ignite a revolution that begins in you.*

On or off the job, your True Work is yours to do. The more of it you do, the more of your Divine Self's potential you will realize, the more God will use you, and the more God will do through you. These experiences of being in service to God will make your soul weep in ecstasy. It will be a success that money and promotions cannot approach. It will be the fulfillment of possibilities previously unimagined. It will be your "pearl of great price" of which Jesus spoke in Mathew 13:43-46. It will be the hidden treasure, the heaven in your midst. True Work is the thing that Abraham Lincoln, John F. Kennedy, Reverend Doctor Martin Luther King, and Jesus found worthy of death. To do the will of Him who sent us, that is the Work, regardless of the job.

This Book

When my book coach suggested that I write this book in the conversational tone of an interview and called it an interview book, I was skeptical. I had never heard of an interview book, but soon I discovered that this format is a powerful tool for communicating complex information in an understandable and actionable way. Trust the process and together we will penetrate the depths of the experience of activating Divinity on the job. This book is an ignition switch, intended to ignite a revolution that begins in you.

The motto "money over man," a theme that has fueled much of the world's oppression (racism, sexism, homophobia, ageism, etc.) and progress, and corrupted many of its ideas and systems (patriotism, religion, communism, capitalism, and socialism to name a few); will reverse itself when we reverse ourselves. This book is designed to shift you into reverse. It will shift you from doing the work of your job to using your job to do your True Work, the work God has positioned you to do.

This is the way the world changes – not when you find a different job, but when you make your job different, by making yourself different on the job!

Like everyone in the world, no matter your story, no matter your race or background, or tribe, you have been exposed to poisonous ideas. Events like slavery, war, and environmental abuse arise out of poisonous ideas. These ideas provide some with money and power, but lethally impact others. Through rationality, patience, and persistence in time, the mind may detect the poisonous nature of an idea, but the heart knows immediately! That is why this is a revolution of the heart. When the heart filters ideas, it easily separates the wheat from the chaff.

My intention in writing this book is to change the world by inspiring and empowering the best and the brightest to become the most spiritually fulfilled, Divinely expressed, and successful. Nice words, but what does this mean? Who are these brightest and best? Well, if you are reading this book, you are!

My prayer is that this book lands in the hands of those for whom it is intended; those who can and will use it to ascend, those who will use it to transform work, its outcomes, and the workplace, nationally and globally. I AM creating this book to be a launching pad for ALL people, who are willing to experience *I AM @ Work*, who are willing to activate deep internal energies and to unleash the Divine Self they are destined to become. If this book has come into your life, decide right now that you are the best and the brightest and that you will do what needs to be done to release the false and reveal the true, Divine Self. My experience has demonstrated that jobs are fertile soil for spiritual growth.

> *Our Divine Self disrupts our false life, so prepare for disruption.*

Jobs thrust us into wanted and unwanted intense experiences that shape our trajectory. Each decision we make, each thought we think, each action we take is a choice point. Practicing spirituality on the job prepares us to make the choice, to answer the call, and to say a loud "yes" to God, the truth, the Divine Self. Our "yes" grows us and the people around us. More importantly, it changes the landscape at the jobs we work and the careers we occupy. This impacts the products and services produced and provided, and it impacts every person and situation that is collaterally connected to those products and services.

Integrating spirituality into life on the job adds to satisfaction and success, and it leads to Divine Identity and fulfillment. There is an itchy, tight, painful discomfort that grates and gnaws at us when we are out of spiritual alignment and working as impostors. If we pay attention and explore that pain, it operates like a sander and smooths away the false inconsistencies, revealing more of the Divine Self. Our Divine Self disrupts our false life, so prepare for disruption.

The good news is that even as it disrupts the old, Divine Self positions us to experience the new. It energetically attracts new situations that grow our ability to express Divinity through True Work. The success stories in this book will show you what that process looks like.

My prayer is that they inspire you to grow and to discover what it can look like for you!

Heart connected and Divinely evolved—that is the world we are creating together here. So, I have one request. When the book works for you, when you activate your Divine Self, pass it on! Sell it if you want! Get this information out there. The goal is not money, bestseller status, fame, or fortune. Those would be nice, I admit. But the goal is greater. The goal is global elevation. If together we work our spiritual practices, we can and will make it happen!

Aiding me in the process of developing the interview content was Sensei Subira Folami, an invaluable member of my book development team, and a dynamic force!⁴ Sensei Subira is a speaker, author, reverend, spiritual life coach, and martial artist who holds a 2nd-degree black belt in American Kenpo. In her book, *How to Transform Wounds to Wisdom and Create a New Life*, Subira explores the ways that our most painful life experiences catalyze our transformation.

She has sat at the feet of some of life's most painful situations and teaches others the healing power hidden in such experiences. Subira has overcome childhood abuse and homelessness. In 2012, she faced down an aggressive form of breast cancer, marshaled her inner strength, and allowed herself to be transformed and transfigured through six months of chemotherapy, thirty-three rounds of radiation, and a double mastectomy. It was incredible to watch as she grew through cancer rather than shrinking from it.

While navigating breast cancer treatment, Subira began serving thousands of people through her life message of transformation via daily YouTube videos and Facebook posts. Subira's passion and purpose is to guide enlightened entrepreneurs through the process of leveraging their stories of transformational life experiences so they can serve more deeply. Like me, Sensei Subira was ordained at the Inner Visions Institute for Spiritual Development under the distinguished tutelage of master life coach, ingenious spiritual teacher, world-renowned speaker, best-selling author, radio and television personality, Reverend Doctor Iyanla Vanzant.

Sensei Subira is my friend, my sister, and a spiritual genius in her own right, meaning she is a person who allows her Divine Self to have its perfect way with her and her life, and she causes or allows herself to grow from whatever events occur. She also unfailingly, persistently, and consistently takes massive action on the urgings of Spirit.

I am honored to have worked with Sensei Subira and have been encouraged by her through this process. I am proud that we are of one tribe!

Book I

NOW

Chapter

Declare Your Authority

Practice is the supreme teacher.

~ Publilius Syrus ~

The only genuine proof of this wisdom is experience itself.

~ Kabbalah ~

If you have not lived through something, it is not true.

~ Kabir ~

Many people in life wait! They wait for authorization, permission, certification, or recognition. They wait for someone or something to tell them they are allowed to be what they want to be and allowed to do what they feel guided to do.

> *Declare the authority God has given you.*

Authority comes from God! The first message of this book is to declare the authority God has given you.

Be and do as God has authorized you to be and do. Declare your authority and watch the world conform to your declaration!

I do not know that I have ever heard someone called an expert in spirituality at work. In fact, I may be the first to lay claim to that title. By the power of my I AM, I claim it. I AM an expert in spirituality at work. I claim this title due to my personal experience practicing spirituality on the job, and experiencing spiritual oneness, Divine Self, and soul fulfillment as a result of doing my True Work. I also claim this title because by coaching, counseling, advising, and teaching others to apply spiritual laws on the job, I have supported others in meaningfully changing their lives and their experiences with Spirit on and off the job. I have been taught many things from many fine institutions of higher education, and many teachers and mentors; however, my expertise in spirituality at work predominantly stems from working in challenging workspaces that demanded spiritual intervention and alignment. Experience has been my teacher and Spirit has allowed me to cull from my experiences principles and strategies that I can offer others.

I AM an expert in spirituality at work. I am not an expert in your relationship with Spirit. Only you and the God of your understanding have that expertise. Though I will offer tools, tips, and transformational tales, it will be grace, grit, and your own readiness that govern the outcomes you experience.

Your first tip is to notice what I did here. I took the experiences God gave me, treated them as a gift for myself and others, explored and culled from them the learning, wisdom, and growth available, then I claimed victory over the experiences by applying my I AM power and by declaring my expertise. You too can do this!

Are there experiences in your life that God has offered you? Perhaps there are painful experiences you have suffered through and rejected. Maybe you have had experiences that felt like failures. These experiences are your gift. If you accepted that these experiences were on your path for a reason and explored that reason, you may find that you too have experiential expertise through which you can benefit the world!

Now, as we begin our first set of interview questions, you will have the opportunity to get to know me a little better and to discover some of the experiences that inspired this book.

The Interview Begins

Sensei Subira: Hello, everyone, and welcome to *I AM @ Work: Unleashing the Power of Divine Self on the Job*. My name is Sensei Subira, and I am talking with Reverend Kelli Jareaux, an expert in spirituality at Work and an attorney.

In this exchange, Reverend Kelli will share her extensive knowledge and experience. Her goal is to allow every person who wants to experience Divinity at work to do so, to discover their True Work, and to learn how to advance it at any job.

Reverend Kelli, tell us why this book is important to you.

Reverend Kelli: This book is important to me because it is a part of my True Work! True Work is what we all are here to do. I look forward to sharing my experiences, and I share them with the hope that my experiences will transform the work-life of all who read this book.

Sensei Subira: I share that hope!

Now, my first set of questions is about your background and experience. We want readers to understand who you are, where you are coming from, and how you relate to where they are right now. Then we will jump to the main areas where people have challenges when it comes to experiencing God on the job, allowing readers to understand how to get past the ideas that prevent so many people from having the experience of God they desire.

So, tell us a little bit about yourself, your background, education, and experience in spirituality and the legal arena. Reverend Kelli, when did you get started as an attorney?

Reverend Kelli: I graduated high school and went to college at Howard University, and then to law school at Georgetown University Law Center. I had a few summer jobs in college and law school, but then immediately after law school, I directly entered my first legal job, which was at a Washington DC law firm.

Sensei Subira: Which law firm?

Reverend Kelli: To maintain anonymity for my clients and the law firm, I will not name it, but it was a respected firm with offices in multiple locations throughout the country. I specialized in administrative investigations. I will not identify the industries. I will just say that most of the clients were household names. My goal and dream is that one day every one of my past and current clients will encourage their employees to implement the tools in this book.

Sensei Subira: That is a great dream, Reverend Kelli. Now, how long did you work for the first firm?

What if more of the energy devoted to profits and strategies was devoted to creating good in the world?

Reverend Kelli: I worked there for a little over ten years. It felt amazing at first! My parents were both blue-collar workers, and when I started at my first law firm job, I believed that my working conditions and salary as a first-year associate were significantly better than what my parents experienced even at the height of their careers. Since I was programmed to want to do better than my parents, I felt good about my position. And the money! It was mind-blowing to make that much money my first year on the job. But also, I felt a lot of pressure to do whatever I needed to do to maintain the privilege of my position.

I have been practicing law for almost 30 years. In that time, I have dealt with and looked into the internal operations of all sorts of corporations. My experiences caused me to ask: what would the world look like if more of these heads of industry were coming from a God-grounded and God-centered space? What if more of the energy devoted to profits and strategies was devoted to creating good in the world?

Or, at the least, what if the hearts of more people in the workplace were firmly grounded in Spirit, rather than in corporate culture or corporate motivations, such as making money for shareholders? What if more of the shareholders themselves were grounded in Spirit and made doing good the highest priority?

I have had a keen interest in spirituality since I was a young girl writing morality plays at Allen Chapel AME Church in my small town of Galesburg, Illinois. I went to Catholic School a couple of years and was in awe of the ceremony and ritual, especially confession. I had a number of spiritual experiences as a young girl that kept me in close contact with God as a presence in my life. Most significantly, I can remember my grandmother Lola, who I called Nanny, reading her Bible, and rocking in her rocking chair. And I can remember her taking me to a local Baptist church where people became filled with Spirit and screamed and then fainted. At the time I was afraid, but I never forgot it, and it created in me an intense desire to understand the power and mystery of Spirit.

As an adult, I continued to explore and experience God. But it was my job that moved me toward a deeper spiritual connection. There came a time when I realized that something was missing on my job. I thought I had everything that the American dream promised, everything I was supposed to want, everything that was supposed to satisfy and fulfill me. Still, I was not satisfied, and most definitely not fulfilled! I knew there had to be more. When I reached that point, I decided to do a deeper dive into spirituality, and I explored that in a lot of ways, but most significantly through Inner Visions. I also trained with Unity and attended courses through Unity's school, at Unity Village.[5]

Sensei Subira: So, you are, in fact, an ordained minister. Tell us more about that and about Inner Visions.

Reverend Kelli: Inner Visions Institute for Spiritual Development, known as IVISD, is a school for coaching and spiritual development. It was founded by Reverend Doctor Iyanla Vanzant, who is a best-selling author, as well as a renowned television personality and life coach. She began the school and personally taught attendees. I was in one of the first IVISD graduating classes.

Sensei Subira: So, how long did it take to finish the program, and what did you study?

Reverend Kelli: It was a four-year program. The first two years were geared toward personal healing and spiritual development, exploring myself and my relationship with God. There is a coaching component in that, a component geared toward discovering your own issues and cleaning up your own life. The training taught me how to clean up the past, experience the present, and co-create a desired future without so much spiritual debris. After the first two years, I began the ministerial program, which was another two years, and then I did a one-year teaching apprenticeship at the school.

Sensei Subira: So, you taught what you learned?

Reverend Kelli: Exactly!

Sensei Subira: What class or course did you teach?

Reverend Kelli: I have taught many spiritual classes. At IVISD, I taught people how to activate the universal laws and principles that underlie the Scriptures from the Bible and other Sacred Texts. No matter the religion, most people reflect on Scripture from the literal words on the page, giving the Scripture a literal interpretation. My class called Practical Metaphysics taught students universal laws and principles and how to align with them and embody them as we co-create our lives with Spirit. This year I am returning to IVISD to teach again. For me, it is so important that we support one another and go beneath the surface of life to discover the truth. As you know, Subira, even when it comes to Sacred Text or Scripture, you and I could read the same words and derive from it two different, valid interpretations—interpretations that are correct for us, for what God is saying to us at that moment. And so, I love teaching people how to align with universal principles and spiritual law and how to read and draw from Scripture and Sacred Text, what Spirit has to say to them at a given moment in time.

Sensei Subira: I understand exactly what you mean!

Now, you were ordained through the IVISD program, correct?

Reverend Kelli: Yes. I also have another ordination, which I had before I attended IVISD. I attended IVISD because I wanted a second ordination, probably because having gone to law school, I was used to being trained through reading books and having instructors. My first ordination was not an ordination like that. I wanted my second ordination to be through an organization that trained me and gave me books to read. That was the way I was accustomed to learning. I had no idea that IVISD would trigger vast, multi-dimensional growth that largely lived far outside the books we were reading.

Sensei Subira: That is so true! That was my experience at IVISD!

Sensei Subira: Let us talk about some of your work experiences. What are some of your relevant experiences with God on the job that may support readers who are looking to experience their Divinity at work?

Reverend Kelli: One of my first experiences was a realization. I realized that who I was as a person often seemed to be at odds with who I was being asked to be on the job. The conflict between the authentic me and the me the job needed me to be was a painful experience each time it occurred.

Just as an example, I am a Black woman, and at one point, my job assigned me to work on a discrimination case. My assignment was to draft a report advocating for a release from administrative reporting responsibilities. My job was to look at the facts and write a persuasive document arguing that the client now was compliant. I was not comfortable agreeing to the assignment without knowing whether the facts definitively supported an argument that the client was compliant. This kind of conflict of conscience happens a lot with lawyers.

Part of a lawyer's job is to put the best face on the case that is handed to us. But, because discrimination laws were put in place to protect people like me, I felt uncomfortable putting the best face on such a case.

Spirit supports us in positioning ourselves to win!

This was my very first test on the job. It was a test that I would either fail by becoming what the job had the capacity to make of me, or pass by being grounded in my True North, my

True Employer, God, and standing for what I knew to be correct for me. So, I had to go within and choose.

Sensei Subira: What did you do?

Reverend Kelli: Spirit supports us in positioning ourselves to win!

Often, we know what we need to and want to do, but we do not know how to do it without suffering a consequence on the job. As a young associate, my power to determine my assignments was virtually non-existent. Refusing work or declaring that I would not or could not do what was being asked of me would not have gone over well. The penalty could have been that I would be viewed as a prima donna and not taken seriously, or that I would not be assigned work and would be unable to bill hours. Billing is the lifeblood of a law firm associate.

Sensei Subira: So, you were kind of in a no-win position. I know what that is like.

Reverend Kelli: Yes, I was. I needed Spirit to reveal to me how I could say "no" while appearing to say "yes" and still preserve my relationship with the assigning partners. Through my experience, I came to understand the secret of saying "no," while appearing to say "yes." This magic formula served me well for the next nine years of my career at the firm. It is discussed generally in Book II (Tip No. 4); yet, its importance cannot be overemphasized. Here is the detailed formula.

The Magic Formula

1. Seek the guidance of a high-level, uninvolved third-party. Do not ask them to intervene. Say, "I want to handle this myself!" Ask them for guidance on how to navigate your situation. Make sure it is someone who knows the company, knows the players, and is themselves well respected. Ask them to keep it confidential and provide no names, be ambiguous, and express your earnest desire to do the assignment. State your conflict (make sure the person you choose is a person you believe has their own True North and moral compass) and ask if they have ever had a similar challenge. Having

them tell THEIR story increases your bond with them and allows them to tap into the truth from the perspective of EXPERIENCE, not what they THINK you should do. This person is your backup advocate in case your effort to say "no," while saying "yes," fails.

2. Figure out what you are willing to say "yes" to and/or the conditions that would need to exist for you to say "yes." These will become components of your "yes." So, instead of a simple "yes," your answer will become a "yes, and." The, "and," will include all the conditions necessary for your "yes" to become a real "yes," rather than a veiled "no."

3. Say yes to what you are willing to say yes to and ask for support in resolving the conditions that obstruct a full yes.

Sensei Subira: Okay, tell us what that looked like in your situation.

Reverend Kelli: What I discovered that I could say "yes" to was producing a factually accurate report. I said "yes" to writing up the facts, and they (the assigning partners) agreed to help me resolve my conditions by getting someone else to add the adjectives and do the persuasive piece. Because I was a young associate, my real job was gathering, distilling, and analyzing information. So, they were open to me writing it up factually since someone more senior would have had to edit and hone my advocacy anyway. I also let them know the reason for my request, and as I was operating in alignment with Spirit and my integrity therewith, instead of being penalized, I became more respected (respect is not promotion, and promotion is not always success, but to me, promotion without self-respect is never success). So many people are focused on permanence, not purpose.

> *So many people are focused on permanence, not purpose.*

They want to be with their employer permanently (or at least until they have a better job), but this is not a permanent universe. Everything in this universe is temporary. If you are so intent on trying to hold on to your job, or anything else for that matter, that you surrender all of who you are, you will miss the opportunity to become all of who you are meant to be, which is an opportunity provided only by standing in your purpose.

Employees constrict themselves into a box by pretending to be what they think their employer wants them to be. This prevents them and their employer from growing into what God would have them be. Does that make sense?

> *The Truth of who I AM must come to work when I do.*

Sensei Subira: Absolutely!

Reverend Kelli: The Truth with a capital "T" is that I was with my employer to have a Divine impact. The Divine design, my Divine purpose for being on the job, could only be authentically executed if I was working as my authentic Self, not as an automaton unquestioningly doing what I believed my employer would have me do. In any job situation, I believe that I am Divinely positioned with my employer to bring the change that I AM. Therefore, the Truth of who I AM must come to work when I do.

Sensei Subira: That makes perfect sense. I love that you said, we are focused on *permanence* instead of *purpose*. I love that.

Reverend Kelli: Absolutely!

Decoding Your Work DNA

Sensei Subira: So, Reverend Kelli, you were successful in combining your spiritual and professional personas?

Reverend Kelli: I did not get it right, right away. What a work culture sometimes does is change an employee's sense of self. The employee once viewed himself or herself as "I." Being an employee of the company slowly shifts the employee's perspective from that of an, "I," to that of a, "we." The employee begins to see himself and the company as one.

"I," is Divine Identity. When pairing or combining our "I" with another "I," that pairing and combining should be done consciously. To abandon our "I," is to abandon our Divine Self. Many employees do this and take on a, "we," that they do not fully understand.

Most corporations and workplaces have beautiful vision statements that say a lot, but their statements often do not translate into a lot in practice. So, when you go to work for an entity, you are in effect co-signing and adding your energy into a conglomeration of energies that you really may not understand.

> *Your True Work begins from the time you land on the planet.*

Often, you may hear yourself espousing the company line, saying, "We believe this" or, "Our policy is such and such." Yet, you may have failed to ask yourself whether you understand where the company's policies come from, who has created the policies and why, and if you really agree with the policies and want to be a mouthpiece for them.

I was as much a product of this kind of thinking as anyone else who falls into an employer's energy vortex might be. It took time for me to understand or "decode" my work DNA. That is what I would advise everyone to do: to decode their work DNA, to find their true calling and True Work, to develop their personal work vision and intention statement.

Sensei Subira: Is there a specific process that you recommend people use for going about doing that, for decoding their work DNA?

Reverend Kelli: There is. Your first job is not your first work. Your work begins from the time you land on the planet.

To decode your work DNA, begin with a look back at what your family's experience was before you were born. Then look at how your entry into that family changed the family culture, structure, and dynamics.

Add to your analysis all your meaningful experiences. When I say meaningful, I am referring to the experiences where you played the hero. You can look at those experiences and see what your work truly is.

For example, when my mom became pregnant with me, my mom and dad were split up. My mom's pregnancy with me (a pregnancy that occurred thirteen years after the birth of my only sibling and one that the doctor told her could not occur) caused my parents to reunite. By entering the family, I unified them.

As time progressed, my work as a unifier continued. I was an extreme daddy's girl! On occasions when my mom would become angry and upset with my dad, I would go back and forth from my mom to my dad, trying to get my dad to apologize, trying to get my mom to accept his apology until I felt like everything between my parents was okay again. My parent's marriage lasted until my dad died in 2015.

Through this and other life events, what I have come to know about myself and my work is that I am a unifier. I can bring people together. I help people reconcile differences. Sometimes this works wonderfully and sometimes it blows up.

> *Once you know the Truth about who you are, you can begin to work in your continuum of genius on the job.*

The blowups are my cross to bear. They are the price I pay to be myself, kind of a consequence of being me, and a beautiful part of being me. I cannot allow the blowups to deter me.

So, for purposes of decoding, you do not discount failed efforts at heroism. The point is that in doing what came naturally in the situation, you caused something big to happen. Once you know the Truth about who you are, you can begin to work in your continuum of genius on the job.

And you will know that you are working in your *continuum of genius* because synchronicities will start to appear.

Sensei Subira: Got it! Your first job where you are paid money is not your first work.

Give us the steps that readers should take to look at who they are on the planet; and, will you also discuss how they can apply what they learn?

Reverend Kelli: What you need to do is look at experiences where you did something, and you had an extreme or unexpectedly good or bad outcome. Such as, where you took a small action and the result was huge. For example, when I was a young girl, we had a neighbor who would come out of her house and scream at all the kids on the block, and, I confess, we would scream back at her. And this was the relationship we had with this woman.

On one occasion when the woman screamed at us, her shouting included telling us that her birthday was the next day. When she said that, I was struck with an idea, and later I said to my friends, "We should make her a cake." We made her a cake and we knocked on the door and she came to the door the day of her birthday screaming at us: "Why are you kids knocking on the door?" But, when she saw that we had this cake she cried. She said she had not celebrated her birthday before. We sat in her house and we ate cake with her, and the entire relationship that we had with her permanently transformed.

Sensei Subira: Wow!

Reverend Kelli: I was not trying to do anything special. I just suggested making a cake for a lady who seemed like she could use one. I did not expect a significant result, but this big thing happened through a ridiculously small gesture of mine because I was in my *continuum of genius* unintentionally acting as a unifier. Does that make sense?

Sensei Subira: Absolutely.

Reverend Kelli: You will be able to piece together your True Work, what you actually came on the planet to do when you look back at your life and find these stories. Look for a small thing with a gigantic outcome or where someone was extraordinarily grateful for something that did not seem to be much at all, or where you experienced strange synchronicity even if the ultimate outcome seemed negative.

Sensei Subira: So, True Work is something that just flows naturally, and it is nothing they need to study or get some sort of official documentation to affirm. It is something that just flows easily. Is that what you are saying?

Reverend Kelli: Well, it does, but you do have to not stop it from flowing. And that is the thing about being in a job. A job can stop you from doing your True Work by influencing you to stop the flow. Only a committed person can do True Work as an employee. By committed, I mean you must be committed to your True Work. When the dictates of the job misalign with your True Work, your commitment is demonstrated by your allegiance to your

True Work. Without profound commitment and devotion to manifesting the Divine Self, pressures of the job may overwhelm. At the risk of telling you another story, let me share something here about synchronicities.

Many years before the story I am about to tell you, I had defended a challenging custody suit over my son. This suit had happened maybe fifteen years before the occurrence of the events I am about to describe. As a result of that custody suit and having raised my son for the fifteen years that followed it, I learned some things. I had become a mediator. When this synchronicity occurred, I was mediating.

As a mediator, my job was to be neutral, meaning not being on one side or the other side. There are specific rules about mediator conduct. In the case I was mediating, something about the man and the energy of the situation took my spirit back to my custody case, and instead of being neutral, Spirit filled my heart with compassion for this man.

Now, this happens to people frequently. Spirit touches their heart and urges them to act, but because they have been so conditioned to believe that work is a place for the head and not the heart, they ignore Spirit's urgings.

At the point in my life when these events occurred, I had experience and training in recognizing and yielding or surrendering to Spirit. So, when I felt this urge, I yielded to it and spoke to the man with a full, open heart.

Instead of strictly following the rules of neutrality, I used my personal experience with my custody case and began to coach him. I told the man of my experience, not the details of it, but that I had faced a custody challenge and thought it would mean the end of the world. I told him I did not let the world end, because I had to parent within the context of the situation that I found myself in. I told the man how I had made sure that each one of the moments I spent with my son was as meaningful as I could make them. And I let the man know that I believed in him and believed that he could respond to the situation he was faced with and not let it become the end of the world.

When I told my story everyone in the room experienced a rare moment, the kind where time seemed to stand still. We experienced this moment, not because of the words that I said, but because of the authenticity, we shared, because of my transparency, and because of the energy of Spirit that expressed through me to him.

Then, this man, who from the start of the mediation had appeared very tough, started to cry, and everyone in the room seemed to experience the transformation.

But the gigantic synchronicity happened when I left the mediation room. Now, remember, my custody case occurred 15 years earlier.

When I left the mediation room, one of the attorneys from the mediation, who had been representing a different party, walked up to me and said: "You probably don't remember me, but I was one of the attorneys who represented the other side in the custody suit over your son. I'm so glad you shared what you shared in the room. I was not sure I recognized you until you told your story. I have often wondered what happened to you. I have left that firm and am on my own doing something different now, as you can see. I'm so glad to hear things turned out well for you and your son."

> We have been invited into the room by God.

Sensei Subira: Wow. Wow.

Reverend Kelli: Yes, this was incredible synchronicity! What this synchronicity allowed me to see is that when I am willing to step outside the rules and do what Spirit is telling me to do at the moment, big things happen, incredible things happen. These things are predestined. Because of who we are, how we are, and what we have experienced, we have been invited into the room by God.

Our experiences are our training. Moving through our life experiences, qualifies us. Our job places us in the position to do what we are called upon by Spirit to do.

But, still, ultimately the choice is ours!

Sensei Subira: I get this! Tell us more.

Reverend Kelli: In a different mediation, I also was guided to step outside the rules. I did. In an individual pre-session conversation, I encouraged the party with custody to yield and allow the other party to visit the child before we conducted our first session. The reason for refusing visits had been minor, and with a bit of coaching, the person was able to rise above it. A visit with the child occurred. All agreed, and it was a great visit. Then, several days passed and I had not heard from either party. I needed to schedule the first joint session, so I reached out but heard nothing back. Finally, I received a call back from the party with custody. What I was told floored me! Before we could even have an actual mediation and days after the visit with his child, the other party died. This time, I was the one in tears!

Sensei Subira: Incredible!

Reverend Kelli: We just never know what God is doing. If we stay inside of the tiny little roles our jobs assign us, we could miss it. We could miss the whole reason we are in the room. We can miss what we are there to do, what God has placed us there to do. Your employer may have put you in the room for one reason, but the reason your True Employer has put you in the room is likely entirely different. Be watchful! Pay attention and be prepared. Then, when the moment presents itself, stand up and do it. Do your True Work!

Be True to God's Truth Expressing Itself as You.

This Is the Path to Your True Work

Chapter

Invite God to Your Job

Man's greatness consists in his ability to do and proper application of his powers to things needed to be done.

~ Frederick Douglass ~

So, whether you eat or drink or whatever you do, do it all for the glory of God.

~ 1 Corinthians 10:31 ~

Commit to the LORD whatever you do, and he will establish your plans.

~ Proverbs 16:3 ~

Remember, it is not a lack of knowing truth that keeps most people from experiencing God at work. It is that the truth they know is competing with all the lies they have come to believe, accept, apply, and live by. When the false is cleared away, the truth becomes apparent. Then all that remains is to choose it.

This next set of questions and answers looks at one of the biggest myths/misconceptions about spirituality at work and how you can move through it.

Sensei Subira: Reverend Kelli, what do you believe is the number one myth or misconception that people, who want to experience their Divinity at work, have about experiencing God on the job?

Reverend Kelli: I think the biggest misconception people have about experiencing God on the job is that they should not experience God on the job, that they should separate God and the job. We have all been told not to discuss religion at work, and not to proselytize at work. We have been taught there are spaces where religion is not allowed. Many have misunderstood this to mean there are spaces where God is not allowed.

Spoiler alert, God is everywhere! Trying to ignore God is just sticking our spiritual head in the sand.

Our awareness of God's Presence is amplified when we invite God in. But attachment to the myth that we are

We can choose a full-time connection with the Presence.

not supposed to mix work and spiritual practice stops us from taking that basic first step. If you think about it, people are spending 8, 10, 12, sometimes even 14 hours at a job daily. People who believe this misconception spend their workday trying to maintain an artificial separation from God. What a waste! Imagine how a person's life would change if instead of spending as many as 14 hours a day separated from their spiritual practice, they spent that time in conscious communion with God.

A long time ago, one of my spiritual mentors, Brother Ishmael Tetteh, told me we do not have a secular life and a spiritual life; we have one spiritual life.[6]

To unleash our Divine Self, we must be willing to experience the fullness of who we are in God, wherever we are and whenever it is. When we try to compartmentalize our life or when we try to keep our practice to moments when we are at home, or when we are at church, or synagogue, or mosque, we lose out. In every moment, we have the option to live in conscious connection with the ever-present Presence of God. We can choose a full-time connection with the Presence.

Sensei Subira: Are there repercussions from the employer for sharing your full self at work?

Reverend Kelli: At most workplaces, it is much better than it once was. At one time the predominant attitude in most workplaces was that spiritual practice was not accepted, but in many places that now has changed. Now, many jobs are welcoming and even introducing meditation and other spiritual wellness practices. Also, many jobs now are accommodating the desire to pray at work by setting aside private space that can be used for that purpose. The world has changed. Besides, there are so many subtle methods of connecting with Spirit that are inconspicuous or invisible. These methods can be implemented even in an unwelcoming workspace. By using the spiritual tools discussed here the opportunity to connect with Spirit at work is open to those who wish to seize it.

Connecting with spirit grounds us in faith in an environment where faith is sure to be needed. The job is one of the most stressful life arenas for many people. God is an answer to that stress. Spiritual connection is the way to ease the burden.

Also, inspiration is necessary for every job. Being able to infuse Divine inspiration into the work being done on the job is going to support you in being your best self and producing your best work. Good work yields positive repercussions.

Sensei Subira: What do you recommend to people who want to experience their Divinity?

Reverend Kelli: They should get to practicing, and again, that does not mean proselytizing. That does not mean trying to win others to your beliefs or to any belief. Although, feel free to give them a copy of this book!

Sensei Subira: Yes, definitely a copy of the book! But seriously, I am glad you clarified the difference between practicing spirituality at work and proselytizing.

Reverend Kelli: Yes. I am talking about experiencing and expressing your spiritual connection with God, the God of your understanding, and connecting with that energy either through prayer or just through feeling the Presence, praise, and an appreciation of the energy of God all around us. This book is not about trying to sell other people on religion.

How To Experience God On The Job

> *Sometimes your proximity is your purpose.*

Sensei Subira: What are some things that you do to experience God at work or to stay in touch with your Divinity at work?

Reverend Kelli: For me, the first thing is to know that by being at work and connecting to Spirit already I am doing God's will. So, how can I explain that? Sometimes people are in jobs and they feel like their job might be a dead-end job, or they feel like their job does not appreciate them or that the work they are doing does not make a real difference.

What I want people to know is that sometimes your proximity is your purpose.

The fact that you are willing to be in that place and be a portal of light, that you are willing to be in a place and allow Spirit to ground itself and express, that might be all that is necessary for you to do. Your energy in the space all by itself might be all you need to do.

But also, you can experience God by enlightening, and I do not mean enlightening others by proselytizing. I mean by ensuring that your light is lit and touching others with your light. Imagine, the boss is about to go and make a critical decision and you bring light into the boss's energy system just through a light-filled greeting. On that day, your hello may be the True Work God intends for you to do.

You are hosting Divinity if you know and are willing to act on Spirit, which likely is something different than what everybody else knows and is willing to act on. If you are not grounded in greed as a thought system and are living and WORKING as an expression of a different thought system, that is a way of experiencing God at work. If you are grounded in the truth of God and consciously tapped into that grounding, it is reflected in every bit of you, from your hello to your smile, to your handshake, to the jokes you laugh at, and the micro-expressions you make when an idea is proposed. All this means that when your boss, or your adversary, or your vendor, or your customer steps into your energy field, he or she might make a different decision just because of your proximity. Does that make sense?

The key thing to do is to know your True Work.

Sensei Subira: Yes!

Sensei Subira: Reverend Kelli, what can a person do if they have fallen into the trap of believing they cannot be spiritual while at work? Is there a way to get back on the right track?

Reverend Kelli: The key thing to do is to know your True Work.

Do the decoding. Figure out your True Work, your purpose, and then go about the business of aligning with it and doing it at your job. For me, when I am experiencing darkness at work, I know my True Work is to bring light to that situation. The key for me is to be myself, to do MY work at the job. I am not out randomly trying to do all the good that needs to be done on the job. I am doing my Divine assignment. I am doing what is spiritually mine to do, on the job or wherever I am.

Sensei Subira: Understood.

Blessing Your Challenges

Reverend Kelli: I want to offer one more thing.

Sensei Subira: Sure.

Blessing Practice

Reverend Kelli: There is a blessing practice that I do. And folks may want to try it. If you have a challenging person who is on your job, pray, affirm, and declare in support of that person. If someone gets the promotion you wanted, know that it is in alignment with God for them to have that promotion, because they received it (no matter how they received it). Pray, affirm, and declare in support of them.

When we begin to pray, affirm, and declare for the most challenging people and the most challenging situations those things resolve themselves, and our faith in God and the frequency with which we invoke Spirit in the workplace grows.

Blessing, in a sense, lovingly weaponizes our prayers.

I have prayed difficult people into promotions, which is to say they moved out of direct contact with me into another space. Note, I did not pray for their demise or curse them. I prayed for their success and my relief from their presence.

Of course, I have also prayed, affirmed, and declared myself out of positions.

So, prayers, affirmations, and declarations are tools we can use and should use generously in support of ourselves, the people we believe are with us, and even and most especially the people we find challenging.

Sensei Subira: That is a different way to look at things.

Reverend Kelli: I had a man, who was on the job with me, and he was a supervisor and the man really took me outside of myself. It was a situation where I felt like I was stepping outside of my Divine Self when I had to be in the man's company. The man inspired profanity. When this man entered the room, he was always disrespectful. I could not understand his behavior.

I started praying to understand him, and I started blessing him, blessing him, blessing him. Soon, I discovered that he was the sole breadwinner in his marriage and was taking care of an infirm wife. My compassion for him grew. Then, just as I was beginning to be unbothered by him, he received a promotion. He had been an onsite supervisor who came to different contracting projects to manage the people who were working on the projects. He then was promoted to an area-wide position, managing the people at his prior tier.

Through my prayers, this man succeeded and was happy and I was happy also. Blessing, in a sense, lovingly weaponizes our prayers, not to do harm, but to bask in Divine (rather than negative) energy. Never pray to harm a person.

Just pray for a resolution to a situation that will be in the highest and best interest of all involved.

Sensei Subira: Okay, lovingly weaponizing our prayers for good. I love it!

*Immerse Yourself in the Divine. Activate
Its Energy at All Times, Everywhere!*

Chapter

3

Do not Believe the Hype: Your Job Is Not Your True Work

"My food," said Jesus, "is to do the will of him who sent me and to finish his work."

~ John 4:34 ~

Your True Work is assigned by your True Boss. You are not at the mercy of those who hire you. You are not doomed to follow their commands mindlessly and heartlessly. Atrocities happen because people believe they have no choice and must do what they are told. In the next set of questions and answers, we challenge the dangerous thinking that says, "I must do everything my employer tells me to do." The work assigned by God is your True Work.

> *God hired you for every job you have ever worked.*

Reverend Kelli: The work a job has assigned may not be the True Work God has positioned you on that job to do. If you start with the understanding that God hired you for every job you have ever worked, that God is always your Undercover Boss, then the dominant task is clear and simple: stay in communication with God and do the work God has assigned.

Failing to acknowledge and perform your True Work leads to feelings of restlessness, frustration, and dissatisfaction. You may exhaust yourself attempting to resolve these feelings by applying physical realm solutions without ever realizing that the cause is spiritual disconnection. Working harder, transferring to different positions within the company, changing employers, and even changing professions, whatever the machination there can be no lasting change without spiritual connection and the clarity it reveals.

Without spiritual connection, one may never figure out their True Work and may persist in a state of perpetual misery, even to the degree of feeling suicidal or homicidal.

Sensei Subira: Will you say more about that?

Reverend Kelli: It is impossible to do your best work if you feel unsettled. When you feel dissatisfied with the work assigned on the job and you believe that work is the basis of your significance to God and the world, you feel unsettled and that feeling nags at you unceasingly. In short, the missing connection results in a lack of fulfillment. Until you have opened to your True Work, you may feel unfulfilled.

It may be a subtle feeling like you have forgotten something, or, a feeling of urgency, like you, are running late. No matter the feeling, it is disruptive energy that prevents you from relaxing. The inability to relax stems from not being who you are. Your True Work is who you are.

Doing your True Work immerses you in Divine inspiration and allows you to experience miracles. In my experience, miracles are inaccessible without an infusion of Divine energy. Miracles occur when you open to your True Work. I have talked about some of the miracles I have experienced already, but all of us have many miracles that we are authorized to facilitate. To be a portal for these miracles, you must step into your True Work. You cannot host miracles while pretending. You cannot host miracles while doing someone else's True Work or while trying to imitate someone else on the job. You cannot host miracles behaving like an automaton or unconsciously doing the job you have been assigned to do. You host miracles when you look beyond the job and find the True Work that is who you really are.

> *Your True Work is your impact.*

Sensei Subira: Help me understand how my True Work is who I am.

Reverend Kelli: Your True Work is who you are much in the same way that whenever hydrogen is present, the impact of hydrogen is present. If two parts hydrogen mixes with one-part oxygen, water is the only outcome. You are elemental. And just as an element and its impact on reality are one, you are one with your impact. What you do when you stand in your authenticity is as certain and precise as what hydrogen does with oxygen. Nitrogen cannot do it! Carbon cannot do it! Gold cannot do it. Only hydrogen can do the work of hydrogen. Your True Work is your impact.

True Work is your effect. You are the only one who can do it. It will remain incomplete if you do not. You will remain incomplete if you do not. And you will feel the impact of being incomplete at a soul level. It will vibrate in ever more reverberating waves the longer it is left unaddressed.

The act of doing your True Work and experiencing its miraculous results is developmental. In other words, you must do it to become your full self. It is creating you, just as you are creating it.

Sensei Subira: I want to stop for a little bit and explore that with you, Reverend Kelli. It sounds like what you are saying is that I go to a job and collect the paycheck and I do the job, but my True Work is not in that office from nine-to-five. Or are you saying that I can experience my True Work while at the job?

Reverend Kelli: True Work definitely can be done on the job and can even be a part of the work the job has assigned if that work aligns with God's will concerning what you are to do at a given time, particularly if it is within your *continuum of genius*. In short, True Work can be done on your job, and wherever else you are Divinely inspired to do it. For example, my True Work in part is as a unifier. I am also a defender of the innocent. I am a person who supports people in reconciling differences to arrive at higher truth using cooperation and creativity. Through doing my True Work, I have discovered more of what my True Work is and more of who I am.

To discover my True Work, I looked through the stories in my personal history and decoded my work DNA. I looked at what I had been doing naturally all my life when addressing situations that confronted me. Seeing what I had done was a way of seeing who I am and honing who I am so I could apply it consciously and in Divine alignment. Once I discovered my True Work, I could simply do it intentionally. Instead of doing it accidentally or by default, I could do it on purpose, surrender to it, and allow God to put me in a position where my innate capacities could be used brilliantly. My jobs as a lawyer, mediator, and coach, and especially as a minister, are fertile ground for the expression of my True Work.

The miracles that occur are not necessarily raising the dead, but they are miracles in the context of what I am doing. Being open to my True Work and receiving Divine inspiration allows me to see what others do not. For example, when mediating I see when people are entrenched in their side of an issue and blind to every other side. I see they are blind to the position they believe is opposed to theirs, and to any and all middle ground or new ground. My True Work in these situations is to spark the vision, allowing the parties to arrive at the best solutions through cooperation and creativity. In this kind of scenario that solution is the miracle. It brings forth an unseen possibility and makes it a living reality.

Sensei Subira: I get that.

Reverend Kelli: Now, I want to discuss a serious issue that stops people from doing their True Work. Many times, not doing your True Work is less a matter of being deaf to the voice of Spirit and ignorant to your True Work, and more a matter of willfully refusing to express what Spirit urges you to express. As mentioned earlier, people tend to choose *permanence over purpose*. They are more worried about how to stay at their job than they are about figuring out what they are really at their job to do.

I reached a turning point in the struggle over permanence when I discovered my "quit power," which is a kind of on-the-job superpower!

I had been on my job for a few years when one of the partners spoke to me very disrespectfully. I went back to my office prepared to resign. I was thinking there was no way I would accept that treatment. I called my mother because that is what made sense to me at the time. I told her, "Mom, I'm planning on quitting my job."

I told her the things the partner had said. I honestly, think it was more about his dismissiveness than his words. But, when I shared my story with her, my mom said, "You know what I did for a living?" My mom was a nurse's aide in a mental institution, and she knew that I knew all too well the story she then recited to me, the story of how a patient had poured out a bedpan on her and then beat her with that bedpan.

Sensei Subira: Oh my God!

Reverend Kelli: So, my mom understood what it meant to be abused on a job. She came from a generation, who like the generations before them sacrificed to financially support family. And, as I have said, I was financially successful at my job. My financial success complicated things because like many first-generation college graduates, I was on, what I call a *legacy quest*. I wanted my success to be a part of my parents' legacy, something they could feel proud of.

Many are on a similar legacy quest, especially those like me who have brown skin or are the first in their family to be well-positioned to succeed, according to American society's cultural definition of success. We all want to make the people who love us proud. This desire can tempt us to compromise who we are.

I was tempted because I loved my parents and I knew what they had sacrificed and what they had put up with. I knew the family history of doing what it takes to secure the survival of the family. I knew my slave grandmother Harriet Robinson had continued a relationship with my slave-owning grandfather Joseph Robinson following the end of slavery to better the sons she had with Joseph and the lives of her brothers and sisters.

> *I became aware that I could quit!*

With all of this in mind, I told my mom, and I will always remember this, I told her: "You and Dad, yes, you did, you worked very hard, and someone beat you with a bedpan. You did all of that, not so your daughter would have to be in this place putting up with this crap. The whole reason you sacrificed as you did was so things could be better for me."

In DC, there are all kinds of vendors who sell things on the street, so I said to my mom, "I'd rather sell peanuts on the street than stay at this job for another day!" As I was speaking, I looked up and saw the partner I had complained about standing in my office doorway. He had heard what I said. So I got off the phone with my mother, and then something happened that had never happened before, the partner apologized.

That day I did not quit, but I had the most empowering and freeing awareness. I became aware that I could quit!

That, regardless of the money, or my parent's legacy, or any fears I had in the past; I had *quit power* and could exercise it, if and when I chose. That awareness transformed my life. Rather than feeling like a draftee, I felt like a volunteer. I was different and my relationship with my job was different. The job realized that too.

Sensei Subira: Let us talk about that a little bit more, because I think everybody who has worked a job where they felt disrespected has wanted to quit but did not quit. Why did you not quit?

Reverend Kelli: I am convinced I did not quit because he apologized. Once I knew I had the power to quit, I was free to be myself, free to do my True Work without fear of repercussions.

Sensei Subira: If he had not apologized, do you believe that you would have quit?

Reverend Kelli: I think I would have because ultimately, I did. It took two more attempts before I got out the door, but I did quit.

Sensei Subira: So, why did it take you three times? What happened?

Reverend Kelli: The second time I quit in the middle of an evaluation, an evaluation in which I had received the highest evaluation I had ever received at the firm.

That time I quit because I had been having a challenging time in my personal life. Part of the reason I was having a hard time was that I had changed practice groups and my years of eating and sleeping at the firm—I once had a pillow and a blanket in the closet near my office—had not paid off. I was working harder than ever and was miserable, so it was no surprise that I would get an evaluation that said I was one of the most valuable associates in the firm. Great, good for me! But my life was trash outside of the doors of the firm. I do not know if I was making some dramatic statement or what I was doing, but I had decided that I was going to quit and I said, "Thanks for the evaluation, but I plan to resign. I don't want to be here anymore." I guess you can say that my resignation was my reciprocal evaluation of the firm.

Sensei Subira: That is hilarious!

Reverend Kelli: It gets better!

I was being evaluated by two people, one of whom was one of my mentors, and he said, "We're going to forget you ever said that." They took me back to my mentor's office and strongly counseled me against quitting. It was good counsel because I had done nothing to set up a foundation for myself to depart. For me, at that point, it primarily was coming from emotions about the fact that my personal life was not going well. So, that was my second attempt to quit.

> *The very awareness that I could quit changed the way I worked because I no longer worked in fear.*

The final and successful attempt involved a conscious invocation of Spirit. I prayed. I said to God, "Show me a sign of what is supposed to happen here." Spirit laid out everything that I needed to say and do to get out of there. It took faith to do what Spirit instructed, but I did. Because I did, when I left the firm, I left very well taken care of and incredibly happy.

My point is that the very awareness that I could quit changed the way I worked because I no longer worked in fear of being fired for not doing this or not doing that, or for doing this or doing that. I lost the stress over what happens if someone does not like what I am doing. I understood that I was willing to be without that job. And, that change of perspective made me start questioning whether the job was worthy of me, instead of questioning whether I was working and behaving in a way that would make the job (the people who controlled the job) feel like I was worthy of it.

Sensei Subira: I know at one point you wanted to leave because of your relationship, at another point it was a lack of respect, but what stopped you from leaving that job? Most people work because they have bills. They have responsibilities. As you said, they fear not being able to meet their obligations and that keeps them trapped in a job where they are not flourishing. And they are not able to unleash their spiritual side, because they feel small, but they put up with feeling small because they have to pay bills.

Reverend Kelli: I understand. You are asking why people should not feel trapped by financial responsibilities.

Sensei Subira: I want you to reassure readers that money is not everything and offer guidance on how they can satisfy their financial obligations.

Reverend Kelli: There is a Scripture in the Bible, 1 Timothy 5:18. Among other things, it says, and I am not quoting it perfectly; but, it in sum says that the worker is worthy of his wages.

God's workers never go unpaid. I have had more financial freedom not working at the job where I was making all the money than I had when I was working there. I was working at the firm making more money than I do now. My yearly salary at that firm was more than I have earned yearly since. Yet, the money I have now, the magic of money that I experience now, is far superior to what I experienced then.

Once another minister asked, "Would you rather have money or have everything you need whenever you need it?" And, I have experienced so much of the second. When I need something, it appears. I can give you a perfect example. Recently, I was complaining a little because something that I needed to do cost more than I wanted to pay. I thought it was going to be $150 and it ended up being $300. I was willing to pay $150 but I did not want to pay the additional $150, even though I believed that what I was buying was in alignment with my path. I was going back and forth in my mind about what to do and went to the mailbox and discovered an unexpected $300 check. It was a check someone was supposed to send me months ago that I did not know I was owed. But, here it showed up right when I needed it, subtle synchronicity reassuring me that the $300 service I was purchasing was in alignment with what I needed to do.

Money always comes, and if money does not come, something else will come that will be like money.

So, these are the kinds of things that happen. People call me up out of the blue wanting coaching because they heard about me from X, Y, or Z. Money always comes, and if money does not come, something else will come that will be like money.

Maybe something I thought I was going to have to pay for is now being provided for free by someone.

If you are willing to stay in alignment with Spirit, Spirit will align your financial supply with your financial need, rewarding you for being faithful instead of fearful.

Sensei Subira: Okay. Let us talk a little bit more. What should people do now that they know they are at the job to do God's work?

Reverend Kelli: It all starts with knowing their True Work. It varies for each person. If you and I are in a room, both working for God, we are not there to do the same thing, nor are we there to do some random good. We are each there to do the specialized work God has set aside for us and created us to do. We must know what that work is to get started.

The first thing a person can do is investigate their heroic past. Look at the moments when things miraculously went better or worse than expected. Look for the authentic moments of appreciation when people appreciated something they did. Look at the moments when they surprised themselves. Like, "Wow, I cannot believe I was able to do this!" Look for moments like that.

Sensei Subira: If they have been derailed by a misunderstanding of why they are on the job, are you saying they can come back by remembering their moments of heroism?

Reverend Kelli: Not exactly. When they are trapped in that misconception and learn the truth, the next step is to open their heart and mind to doing their True Work. It begins with opening and becoming willing. Openness and willingness attract opportunity.

When we stop restricting ourselves and open to our True Work, the genius of our Divinity flows freely. It becomes unobstructed and easy to identify. This is when we should explore it, attempt to understand it, align with it, hone it, and grow it.

After they discover what their True Work is, they should look out for opportunities where Spirit is nudging them to do that Work; and, not just opportunities on the job, but, everywhere. When they do that, they will start experiencing miracles regularly.

Even if the thing that Spirit is asking is a thing you feel like you do not want to take on, if you see that it is within your *continuum of genius*, then trust the God who has set that before you. Like a taxi dispatcher, God sees the entire field of need and arranges for that need to be filled by one He qualifies to fill it. Because you are always moving, there is always going to be an intersection between where you are and what the Divine need is. God will qualify you! You will always be in the right place at the right time. The only question is, will you be open to doing what is rightly yours to do?

Miracles Result When You Are
Open and Willing to Do Your
True Work On or Off the Job!

Chapter

*Worthy Work: Knowing the
Divine Value of What You Do*

*The highest reward for a man's toil is not what
he gets for it but what he becomes by it.*

~ John Ruskin ~

We work to become, not to acquire.

~ Elbert Hubbard ~

*To accept your littleness is arrogant because it means that
you believe your evaluation of yourself is truer than God's.*

~ A Course in Miracles ~

I once had a job with my name on the door, leather lounging chairs for my guests, social events with paid $500-a-plate dinners, and receiving lines for handshakes with the President and First Lady. I resigned from that job. Now, my work is routine. I am unknown. The perks are nonexistent.

Some would say the first job was *success* and that the second job is *failure*. I know better. To unleash the power of your Divine Self at work, you too must know better. You must adopt a higher standard of success. Success for me is a clear conscience and a clean heart.

> *You must adopt a higher standard of success. Success for me is a clear conscience and a clean heart.*

It is exercising my freedom and doing my True Work. It is participating in life and being a contribution. It is unleashing the power of my Divine Self and basking in the experience of God doing its work through me, outcomes notwithstanding. True Work is not about outcomes. It is about the infilling and outflowing of Spirit.

What is success for you?

Understanding your definition of success will focus your mind on what is important to you. Focus gives birth to perspective. Perspective reduces stress. Note, you are focusing on what is important to you, not me, your boss, your spouse, your parents, or anyone else. God put you on the job, not anyone else. My definition of success is my definition. Do not adopt it. Discover your own!

> *Going to work, day-after-day, and feeling inept, underutilized, or undervalued is the death of the soul by a thousand cuts.*

Remember, each of us is significant simply by virtue of being in the world embodying the Spirit of God. Jobs do not create significance. We bring significance to the job by being there and doing our True Work.

The next set of questions and answers will focus on significance.

Sensei Subira: So, Reverend Kelli, let us get right to it. What is the biggest challenge on the job concerning significance?

Reverend Kelli: The biggest challenge is a belief that the job does not make a difference in the company or the world. Some people believe that time spent on the job is time wasted because they believe that their job is insignificant. Going to work, day-after-day, and feeling inept, underutilized, or undervalued is the death of the soul by a thousand cuts.

Each day eats away a little more, bit by bit until there is nothing but numbness. Imagine how miserable and frustrating it is to feel like you are wasting 40 hours or more per week. Imagine how mediocre a job you would do if you felt like your job was a waste of time. This belief hurts job morale and performance.

Sensei Subira: But is it true? Maybe some people work, and from what they see, their job does not make a difference. Why is that a false belief? Do you contend that all jobs make a difference?

Reverend Kelli: Yes! That is exactly my contention.

As we have already talked about, if you are doing the practices discussed in this book, you are significant. If you are unleashing your Divine Self, your presence on the job, doing the job, is the first thing that makes the difference. The fact that you are bringing Divine Energy into the workspace makes a difference. The energy you infuse into the work you do adds significance.

So, no matter how routine the job or the work being done on the job, there is an opportunity to use it to change the world.

Spirit is the energy you bring and the energy you are. Divine Energy is contagious, so anyone who comes in contact with work infused with Divine Energy will be influenced by that energy.

We are energy portals. If I make shoes, and what I bring to the shoemaking process is the energy, "I hate this job. I am so frustrated. These shoes do not make a difference, and I am not getting paid enough." I block my own blessing and anyone who puts on the shoes will step into the energy of my misery, and the shoes will not bless them.

Now, suppose instead that I choose to bless myself and while making shoes I am tapped into my Divine Self, my unique purpose, my purpose for being on the planet; then a person who walks in the shoes will step into a *continuum of genius*, a field of Divinity, and they will be blessed. Anyone who contacts the person wearing the shoes also will be blessed. The people who live with the person who owns the shoes will be blessed, and so on, and so on, and so on!

Jesus spoke to us of mystery and mysticism, stating that heaven is among us, implying this is a world of dimensionality where there is much more to all things than what meets the eye. A shoe is more than a shoe. It is an energy center. What kind of energy does it carry? It depends on what kind of energy it is infused with. So, no matter how routine the job or the work being done on the job, there is an opportunity to use it to change the world.

We can change the world by making shoes if we make them with the right energy.

I want to encourage you to think of your job as your church. Think of it as a place of fellowship where the energy of God is exchanged among employees. See yourself as minister of the church. I say *minister* and not *pastor* because *pastor* sometimes suggests a position of hierarchical authority. This is not about authority or force or preaching at anyone. It is about becoming a living love receptacle, receiving God's love, and a living love offering, transmitting the energy of God's love to others. Certainly, energy can be transmitted by talking and preaching. At work, I encourage you to use a different approach, an approach I refer to as *EDI*.

Sensei Subira: What is *EDI?*

Reverend Kelli: The letters *EDI* are the first three letters of the word *edify*. You want to edify your job and those who work there. To edify is to instruct or benefit, especially morally or spiritually, to uplift your job in the way that a religious painting uplifts those who view it.

EDI

EDI is a shorthand or mnemonic for a way of being that others find irresistible. I do not mean irresistible in terms of enchantment. I mean irresistible in terms of not giving rise to resistance. Resistance is obstructive energy that blocks people from receiving the good available to them. To benefit others effectively, do it in a way that minimizes resistance, and supports them in overcoming resistance. *EDI* does both.

E—*Exude, Emanate, Embody, Explore, and Express.* The primary principle is to edify by example. Be an example of how an individual in any circumstance, in any job, can *embody* their Divine Self and *exude*, *emanate*, and *express* Divinity. Be an example of how they can *explore*, go beyond boundaries, and self-imposed limitations, and think not just outside of the box, but as if the box does not exist. This is your assignment on the job. Anything the job asks you to do is additional.

D—*Do, Demonstrate, Dare, Deliver, Detach, and Discern. Do* act. *Demonstrate* Divinity. *Dare* to do the things that are yours to do in Spirit. When others ask you what they can *do* to activate Spirit in their lives, *deliver* support. *Deliver* on the things Spirit asks of you. *Detach* from the outcome; that is Spirit's concern, not yours! Then, *discern* and allow Spirit to reveal the next most appropriate step.

And *Decline, Disengage, Deny*. *Decline* to engage in negative external and internal behavior, such as negative conversation, gossip, judgment, rumormongering, and deceit. *Disengage* from negative external and internal energy, such as fearmongering, complaining, doubting, and blaming. *Deny* the undesirable.

Denial weakens the hold of negative energies. Denial, in this context, refers to a spiritual technology that nullifies (not the existence of a thing), the power of a thing to negatively impact the circumstances of the person using the tool. Denial activates "no weapon formed against me shall prosper" (even the weapons you form against yourself through your thoughts, feelings, and beliefs). Negative beliefs, doubts, resistance, and fear disempower via the negative action of creativity. You work against yourself by fueling negative creations. *Denial* acknowledges the presence of beliefs, doubts, resistance, and fear and puts that energy to use for positive creative action. *Denial* prophylactically nullifies negative creations and quickens the manifestation of desired outcomes.

Here are a few denials you can use on the job. Say them aloud or to yourself. Or post them in private places, so you can read them often.

- Nothing can interfere with me accomplishing that which Spirit has for me to do. Even doubts, negative beliefs, resistance, and fear energetically cooperate with what God seeks to accomplish through me.

- There is no separation between me and that which I am Divinely destined to accomplish. No matter how they appear, all energies support my True Work.

- All obstacles push me back to catapult me forward to where God desires me to be.

- Creating denial statements is simple. You can choose general or specific denials. The denial statements above are general. A specific denial would target the exact negative belief, doubt, resistance, or fear that you believe to be an obstacle. Like the denial statements below.

- The fear of speaking in public is powerless to derail me. It fuels what I speak through my Divine Self.

- Though time feels limited, in the eternality of God there is infinite time for me to do the things that Spirit would have me do.

- The resistance to this project drives me more deeply into the spiritual realm from which I draw my power to accomplish all things in alignment with God's will.

There are many methods for constructing denials. This is my method.

1. Begin with an acknowledgment of the energy you are seeking to transform or realign. Below I have bolded the acknowledgment words from the denials above.

- Nothing can interfere with me accomplishing that which Spirit has for me to do. Even doubts, negative beliefs, resistance, and fear energetically cooperate with what God seeks to accomplish through me.

- There is no separation between me and that which I am Divinely destined to accomplish. No matter how they appear, all energies support my True Work.

- All obstacles push me back to catapult me forward to where God desires me to be.

- The fear of speaking in public is powerless to derail me. It fuels what I speak through my Divine Self.

- Though time feels limited, in the eternality of God there is infinite time for me to do the things that Spirit would have me do.

- The resistance to this project drives me more deeply into the spiritual realm from which I draw my power to accomplish all things in alignment with God's will.

2. Add a statement denying its power or declaring its powerlessness. In bold below are the statements addressing power or powerlessness from the examples.

- Nothing can interfere with me accomplishing that which Spirit has for me to do. Even doubts, negative beliefs, resistance, and fear energetically cooperate with what God seeks to accomplish through me.

- There is no separation between me and that which I am Divinely destined to accomplish. No matter how they appear, all energies support my True Work.

- All obstacles push me back to catapult me forward to where God desires me to be.

- The fear of speaking in public is powerless to derail me. It fuels what I speak through my Divine Self.

- Though time feels limited, in the eternality of God there is infinite time for me to do the things that Spirit would have me do.

- The resistance to this project drives me more deeply into the spiritual realm from which I draw my power to accomplish all things in alignment with God's will.

3. Finally, add the flip, the words of transformation, and make sure the words include a declaration or invocation of Divine Alignment. We only want to manifest that which is in Divine Alignment; for those things, we will have Divine Support. Below I have bolded the words of transformation, declaration, or invocation from the example denials.

- Nothing can interfere with me accomplishing that which Spirit has for me to do. Even doubts, negative beliefs, resistance, and fear **energetically cooperate with what God seeks to accomplish through me**.

- There is no separation between me and that which I am **Divinely destined to accomplish**. No matter how they appear, **all energies support my True Work**.

- All obstacles push me back to **catapult me forward to where God desires me to be**.

- The fear of speaking in public is powerless to derail me. **It fuels what I speak through my Divine Self**.

- Though time feels limited, **in the eternality of God there is infinite time for me to do the things that Spirit would have me do**.

- The resistance to this project drives me more deeply into the spiritual realm from which I draw my power to accomplish all things in alignment with God's will.

I—*Incite, Initiate, Inspire, and Infuse*. This is about causing Spirit to be expressed through our actions. It is about waking others to the experience of Spirit and *inciting* them to feel the experience of Spirit; *initiating* actions, as Spirit has directed; *Inspiring* those who contact you or the things you do. And, *infusing* it all with Spirit, the energy of God that flows through you.

Sensei Subira: I love it!

Now, if I am someone who has fallen into the trap of believing that what I do does not make a difference or that I am no good at what I do, how can I get back on track?

Reverend Kelli: Begin by using your time on the job to build yourself up mentally and spiritually. While doing your job, you can build yourself up by saying affirmations: "I AM a dynamic center of productivity," "I AM excellent at all that I do," "I AM an instrument through which God delivers the highest good in all situations." And prayers: "Mother/Father God, instill in me discernment, wisdom, and stamina to align with your will and to be a force for good in my life and the world." You can do a one-minute meditation. Start by doing whatever small thing you are willing to do to realign your consciousness.[7]

> *A job that feels like a curse because of its mindlessness is a blessing in that it offers a bountiful opportunity for Divine communion.*

Begin by creating meaning. Make your time on the job meaningful doing whatever works for you. One thing I enjoy is listening to audiobooks. I listen to all kinds of audiobooks through my telephone. When I spend time at work listening to spiritual books, I shift, and that time becomes sacred for me, a time of praise and practice instead of wasted time. A job that feels like a curse because of its mindlessness is a blessing in that it offers a bountiful opportunity for Divine communion.

You can transform forty hours that felt wasted into forty hours committed to sacred practice. Your perceived weaknesses or disabilities in Divine order and Divine timing ultimately may become your greatest assets in God. This is exemplified in Paul's experience as described in 2 Corinthians 12:7-10 (Message Bible Version):

Because of the extravagance of those revelations, and so I wouldn't get a big head, I was given the gift of a handicap to keep me in constant touch with my limitations. Satan's angel did his best to get me down; what he in fact did was push me to my knees. No danger then of walking around high and mighty! At first, I did not think of it as a gift, and begged God to remove it. Three times I did that, and then he told me,

My grace is enough; it is all you need.

My strength comes into its own in your weakness.

Once I heard that, I was glad to let it happen. I quit focusing on the handicap and began appreciating the gift. It was a case of Christ's strength moving in on my weakness. Now I take limitations in stride, and with good cheer, these limitations that cut me down to size—abuse, accidents, opposition, bad breaks. I just let Christ take over! And so, the weaker I get, the stronger I become.

A modern example of this view, minus the whole blaming Satan thing (which I do not cosign), was expressed by Helen Keller, who said: "I thank God for my handicaps, for, through them, I have found myself, my work, and my God."

1 Corinthians 15:58 instructs us to stand firm and let nothing move us, to give ourselves fully to the work of God, and to know that our labor is not in vain. Standing firm and giving ourselves fully to the work of God is the path of significance!

Stir and Stay in Divine Energy;
In God, There Is No Waste.

Chapter

Fearless Office Politics for Spiritual Pros

The greatest devotion, greater than learning and praying, consists in accepting the world exactly as it happens to be.

~ Hasidic Saying ~

Grow antennae, not horns.

~ James Angell ~

What we call human evolution is the awakening of the Divine nature within us.

~ Peace Pilgrim: Her Life and Work in Her Own Words ~

Some people run from place to place, job to job, looking for a perfect external environment. Time is better spent evolving the perfect internal environment. As the saying goes, do not curse the darkness, be the light. When we leave dark places dark, darkness reproduces itself. When we are willing to stay put and light the dark places, change happens, and we begin to spur evolution in the environment around us.

Make yourself a holy contagion.

Spur evolution on the job, evolution within you, and evolution all around you. Use this book and all it offers to make yourself a holy contagion.

The people who work on your job are not your enemies. Your job is not your enemy. You are there to inculcate positive change. Where it is good, you make it better. Where it is troubling, you make it good. I recently heard something that fits perfectly here: you are at your job to encourage an environment where people turn to each other instead of turning on each other. You do that by participation, not by avoidance.

Standing above and seeing through office politics is both a practiced AND an automatic experience.

This next set of questions and answers discusses the path of participation and detachment and encourages you to choose it. Spirit makes working this paradox possible. Participating in work while engaged in sacred practice scrapes away falseness and calls forth your Divine Self. This is the unleashing process.

Reverend Kelli: Office politics are one way of participating. A major misconception exists about avoiding office politics. Spiritual people think they ought not to have anything to do with office politics. Some even believe office politics are beneath them. Office politics are unavoidable. At your job, you are inside the vortex. And no matter who you are office politics will impact you.

Sensei Subira: What should a person do when faced with office politics?

Reverend Kelli: As a person who wants to experience God on the job, what you want to do is stand above the politics and gain from them. You want to use your spirituality to see through the politics and see their impact on the environment around you. The way you do that is to do the spiritual practices already discussed and those that will be discussed in Chapter 7 and throughout the rest of this book.

Sensei Subira: Tell me more!

Reverend Kelli: Standing above and seeing through office politics is both a practiced AND an automatic experience.

The practiced part of the experience is what my spiritual mother, Reverend Doctor Iyanla Vanzant, calls doing your work. The more you do your spiritual practices, the more you start to align with Spirit. Think of spiritual practices as a way of sanding down the areas of misalignment. The more you practice, the more aligned you become. The more aligned you are, the more you ascend above the ordinary way of perceiving situations and begin to see through what appears to be. Seeing through what appears to be, allows you to connect with what is.

> *When we align, we see not the correctness or incorrectness of any gossipy theories, but the heart of the players and the principles in effect.*

Sensei Subira: What is?

Reverend Kelli: What is really happening in the situation. When you are in alignment with Spirit, you can look past personality and see principle. You can determine how you fit into the situation.

Sensei Subira: For example?

Reverend Kelli: Imagine you work for a boss who seems to prefer male employees over you. This boss steers projects away from you. You do not understand. All the work you have done for him has gone well. Others have noticed this trend, and it is a topic of discussion. Some have speculated that it is personal, that he just does not like you. Some have speculated that it is coming down from the boss's boss and that it is happening because the boss's boss is sexist. Others believe your boss is gay and enjoys working with men for that reason. All this information is swirling around. And you can do nothing to avoid the situation because it centers around you! A situation like this can feel overwhelming.

Enter Spirit! When we align, we see not the correctness or incorrectness of any gossipy theories, but the heart of the players and the principles in effect.

Now, assume you have done your spiritual practices. You are in a space of alignment. From a space of alignment, it is clear to you that you have a good relationship with this boss, and he likes you and likes your work. You know it is not that he personally dislikes you, and you are sure he is attracted to you. From the space of an innocent heart, you ask your boss if he is aware that there is talk about him steering work away from you. You ask if he is steering work away from you or if everyone is just mistaken. From this level of alignment, your question elicits the truth. The boss confesses that in the past when he has worked closely with attractive women, rumors of affairs have swirled. He tells you that the last time he worked closely with a woman, one of these rumors made its way to his wife and created tension in his marriage. He apologizes and confesses that his fear of this has possibly subconsciously caused him to steer work away from you. He commits to discontinue this practice, and he does!

Sensei Subira: That is a great example! I like the way you say alignment elicits the truth.

Reverend Kelli: Yes, and even where it does not elicit the truth, you will still be able to get a sense of the truth.

Sensei Subira: Now, it seems like you are talking about three things. First, that office politics exist. Second, that office politics are inescapable. And third, we should not try to escape them. Is that right?

Reverend Kelli: Absolutely right! I call it a strategy of *disengaged engagement*.

Sensei Subira: That is tasty, *disengaged engagement*! So essentially, Spirit is supporting the disengagement and the engagement?

Reverend Kelli: Spirit supports both! Spirit allows us to consciously enter the swirling political morass without being pulled under, pulled in, or overwhelmed. It allows you to stand amid the madness, without going mad yourself. It allows you to be in a disengaged state from the context of human attachment so that you are not attached to outcomes, personalities, stories, personal beliefs, or baggage. And, most importantly, it allows you to be in an engaged state from the context of spiritual energy, an energy that facilitates a right and perfect resolution. Of course, the key here is to not judge the resolution and to have faith that whatever the resolution, IT IS RIGHT AND PERFECT.

We are the lightning rods that invite Spirit in. We are the crowbars that pry the doors open.

Sensei Subira: But Reverend Kelli, what about the sticks and stones philosophy. Why not just ignore the politics, ignore the gossip, or what people say about us? What is the value of engagement?

Reverend Kelli: Great question! Let us stop for a minute and talk about what office politics are. I define office politics as the metamessages that govern decision making within the office. Here, I am not using the term metamessage in the traditional sense, I am using it to refer to the messages communicated through rumor, through gossip, through an awareness of the views and desires of those who wield influence; and, here is where we come in, through the profound engagement of the spiritually aligned. Office politics are another way we contribute to the spiritualization of the job.

Remember, we are in our position so that we may act as agents for God. We are not on the job simply to progress or promote ourselves, or even just to have a platform for doing our True Work; we are also there to be agents of change. We are on the job to be spiritual alchemists, to change the nature of the job and the workplace by grounding it in Spirit. We are the lightning rods that invite Spirit in. We are the crowbars that pry the doors open.

We are there on the job to give Spirit a seat at the table. That means that we must not withdraw from any table. We must engage to give voice to Spirit.

Does that make sense?

Sensei Subira: So much sense!

Sensei Subira: Reverend Kelli, are there office politics at every job, or are these just for folks who work in big corporations or law firms?

Reverend Kelli: Every workplace is political. Even families are political. I know a young man who chose a college major that would have positioned him squarely in the corporate world. After studying the ways of corporations for four years, he decided that he wanted to live simply. He took a job as a cashier in a small store. For the first week, he was doing very well and was happy. In week two, he was still doing well, but while some were impressed with his excellence, others were threatened by it. By the third week, he learned that the manager and assistant manager were at war with one another and that his excellence had been used by one as a weapon against the other.

The moral of this story is that no matter what kind of job you have, you will be confronted with office politics, and you will need to know how to respond when you are. God is always the best response!

Sensei Subira: Amen to that, Sis! Do you have any kind of quick way for a person to align?

Reverend Kelli: I do have a flash alignment process that can move a person from chaos to Spirit in 60 seconds or less. I call it Breathe and Bless. It is a lifesaver! First, inhale and silently sound the name you use for God, such as Jesus, Holy Spirit, Allah, or if you do not choose to use a name, just mentally sound the word, peace. Next, exhale and silently recite a blessing over the chaotic situation. Then, flash a picture of the blessed outcome across your mind during the pause after the exhale. Repeat the process for a minute or until you feel the sense of alignment move over you.

Sensei Subira: Okay, Reverend Kelli, I have two questions. First, how do we bless the situation? If I am having a political problem at work, how do I bless it? And second, how do I feel the sense of alignment you are describing? What does it feel like?

Reverend Kelli: Perfect! My favorite way of blessing is through declarations, such as, the Holy Spirit of God is now blessing and resolving in a right and perfect way all experiences on my job that cause me stress. Another way is to simply use words of blessing, such as I bless my boss and all matters at my job. I also like to use "may" statements. Like, "may all matters at my job be clear, understandable, and uncomplicated." So that is how to bless a situation.

As for the second question, trust me, you will know. It is the difference between a windstorm and a calm day, the difference between racing thoughts and a calm mind, between confusion and clarity. It is peace, clarity, awareness, detachment, surrender, and certainty, in mind and body, and Spirit, as it experiences oneness.

Sensei Subira: What else do we need to know about office politics?

Reverend Kelli: Well, we have not talked about fear. This is significant. Once we begin to see, fear may tell us to close our eyes. It can be painful and frightening to see what is going on at the job. You may want to close your eyes and say, *Oh No, No, No. I cannot believe what I am seeing.* Do not do that! Do not close your eyes to the truth. Open your eyes. Activate your spiritual energy, and then use your energy field to influence things for the better.

Engage Political Situations
Fearlessly. God Trumps Politics.
Get Aligned and Stay Aligned!

Chapter

6

Activate the Ultimate Work Mindset

*We choose our joys and sorrows long
before we experience them.*

~ Khalil Gibran ~

The mind is never right but when it is at peace with itself.

~ Seneca ~

*The eternal is not attained by rites and rituals, by pilgrimages
or by wealth. It is attained only by conquest of one's mind.*

~ Yoga Vasistha ~

Three Biblical instructions are the foundation for the information offered in the next set of questions and answers. Commonly Mantra is thought of as a part of Eastern spiritual traditions; however, the Bible subtly directs the use of Mantra also. Matthew 6:22 and Luke 11:34 promise us that if we keep our eye single, our whole body will be filled with light. Mantra is a process that supports this single-minded focus. In 1 Thessalonians 5:17, we are instructed to pray unceasingly, and in Mark 11:24, to pray believing we have received that which we have asked for. These three instructions are the basis for the mindset referred to here as Mantra.

Sacred sound and the sacred meaning of the words sounded are key elements of Eastern Mantra practice. The energy embedded in the Mantra, accumulated from its repetition and the positive intentions of those who have repeated it for generations is also important. Here when the term "Mantra" is used it does not refer to traditional Eastern Mantras, but you are free to substitute and use Eastern Mantras in your practice if you prefer.

Here the term "Mantra" is used generically to mean a statement or thought to focus the mind, a statement or thought that will accumulate energy and gain power with repeated use, and a statement that will become automatic and sound itself in your mind, day after day, hour after hour, providing you with powerful support as you pursue your job and when you are doing your True Work. Below I will recommend a specific Mantra and tell you how you can customize it or another Mantra to meet your needs.

Sensei Subira: Now, let us talk a little bit about mindset. Is there a particular mindset that is more amenable to experiencing God on the job? What mindset will empower readers to integrate spirituality into their work for more satisfaction and success?

Reverend Kelli: Readers should adopt a mindset that says, God is my True Employer, and expressing Divinity is my True Work.

That is it; readers should use this statement as a Mantra! God is my True Employer and expressing Divinity is my True Work. If they use this Mantra, then the things happening around them that would otherwise seem to be stressful and contrary to the sentiment expressed in the Mantra will diminish in importance and they will be able to stand above them.

Sensei Subira: When you say, use it as their Mantra, what does that mean?

Reverend Kelli: When I use the word Mantra, I am using it in a very generic sense. I am talking about customizing a statement of support and using it in a way similar to the way traditional Mantras are used.

Sensei Subira: And how is that?

Reverend Kelli: The way I am recommending that it be done aligns with three Biblical principles. One principle encourages unceasing prayer. The second asks that we pray believing that we will receive. The third directs us to maintain a single eye to fill our body with light.

Sensei Subira: Okay, unceasing prayer, believe we will receive, and a single eye.

Reverend Kelli: Exactly! Principles that are repeated across the spectrum of different religions are the kind I find most valuable. In selecting what draws me closer to an experience of oneness with Spirit, I will use whatever I find in any spiritual tradition that is effective. I will customize it in any way I need to so that it works for me. If there is nothing out there, I will connect with Spirit and invent something.

Sensei Subira: It sounds like your personal spiritual practice is very flexible and eclectic.

Reverend Kelli: It absolutely is! I value this. My allegiance is to experiencing God, drawing nearer and deeper, growing. I am going to do what that requires. When one method stops working, I am willing to surrender it and welcome a new method.

Sensei Subira: I think that is important, and I want to get back to that, but first, I want to hear more about how to use Mantra.

Reverend Kelli: Let me offer a little background first. By that I mean, background about how I selected the techniques to include in this book. I chose them for ease, efficiency, and economy. My entire ministry, the GROW Continuum, is about easy access to God. I believe a spiritual practice is meant to uplift the practitioner, not burden them. I believe my mission as a minister is to provide methods and

We are unique spiritual beings, and our practice can be just as unique.

mechanisms that make our love of God actionable 24 hours a day. I am focused on making spiritual practice portable and timesaving. I am also focused on offering a practice and belief system that allows practitioners to meet God where they are. We are unique spiritual beings, and our practice can be just as unique. There is nothing wrong with that.

We do not have to do what everyone else does. It is more important for us to do what works for us. In my view, this is the same for restricted and permitted behaviors. There is a Scripture in the Bible that says all things are allowed, but not all things are beneficial. Another says the New Covenant will be one in which sins are forgotten and God writes his laws upon the heart of the individual. The New Covenant arrived with Jesus. I believe that Jesus demonstrated the intimate, constant connection with God that we are to aspire to, a relationship that will grow and deepen us spiritually and will expand human experience and understanding of the Divine, a relationship in which we infuse every area of our lives with spirituality.

> *You have one life. Inviting a deeper awareness of God into any aspect of it invites that deeper awareness into every aspect of it.*

I am going to go off track for a moment here because I promised to address family relationships and the relationship with the significant other. Here is a good place to do that. My point here is a simple one. It is critical that before you enter the doors of your job, you have taken a few moments to infuse spirituality into your family relationships and your relationship with your significant other or others. Spiritual practice, like negativity, is contagious. The more you practice it in one area of your life, the more you will experience positive effects, and the more likely you are to expand its practice into other areas of your life. This book is about igniting your I AM energy and unleashing your Divine Self on the job but it is also a course in how to create a robust, dynamic, efficient, and portable spiritual practice that you can apply in any area of your life. Your life is whole. Approaching it in secular and spiritual fragments does you a disservice. You have one life.

Inviting a deeper awareness of God into any aspect of it invites that deeper awareness into every aspect of it.

In other words, the impact of your practice will naturally spread across the various areas of your life. But you can choose to be intentional. You can choose to adapt these practices and apply them to any area of your life.

I recommend that you adapt and apply these work practices to your family relationships and your relationship with your significant other or others. Relationships are likely to contribute to on-the-job stress if left unattended. Adopting a Mantra mindset and practice is perfect for use in supporting family and significant other relationships.

> *God is my True Employer and expressing my Divinity is my True Work.*

Now, let us get back to the Mantra itself. The one I created for us to work with is this: "God is my True Employer and expressing my Divinity is my True Work."

This can be altered or expanded to cover family and significant other relationships. You may create a Mantra like, "God is family, and I express my love of God through a love of family." Or, "God is my lover, my true spouse; I express my love of God through a sacred relationship with my right and perfect significant other." Note, significant other is not the term I prefer here. I suggest you customize the Mantra to whatever language you use to identify your significant other. Just make sure the language does not trigger other negative associations.

Sensei Subira: Negative associations?

Reverend Kelli: Yes, this probably goes without saying, but if you refer to your significant other with terms that have both negative and positive connotations, such as my "old lady," you probably would want to include a different term in your Mantra. Choose a term that is similarly familiar and comfortable for you, but one that does not trigger a second derogatory meaning. The Mantra should sound like your own inner voice, so customization is preferred.

You always want the clearest, cleanest message possible, not a message that triggers resistance. If you use language that is foreign to you, your mind may reject the message, experience some incongruence, or at least hesitate before absorbing the energy. Ideally, you would like to avoid this and create a Mantra that is very compatible.

Sensei Subira: So, are folks creating three different Mantras?

Reverend Kelli: That is a possibility. Another possibility, and the one I recommend, is to combine all three areas of concern into one Mantra that can be used at home and work. For example, the Mantra, "God is my True Employer and expressing my Divinity is my True Work," can be expanded and altered to, "God is my truth and expressing my Divinity on the job, with family, and in my relationship is my True Work."

Sensei Subira: Once we have the perfect Mantra, what do we do with it, and how does it relate to the three Biblical principles: pray unceasingly, pray believing you will receive, and keep your eye single to light your whole body?

Reverend Kelli: Thanks for getting us back to that.

> *Say it enough that when you are not saying it, like an earworm, it is saying itself in your mind.*

Your Mantra is to be your unceasing prayer. It is to be repeated and repeated and repeated. It is to be repeated with the deep belief that what is spoken is true and has already been done. In other words, it is to be prayed believing it has already been received. This process of repeating a single sacred statement with a deep and abiding belief in its truth is a process that makes the eye single. So, you see how the use of the Mantra hits upon every one of the three Biblical instructions that I mentioned.

Sensei Subira: I do! How long do we need to say the Mantra?

Reverend Kelli: The short answer is *always*. Say it always! Traditionally, Mantras are recited 108 times at least once daily and there is a sacred aspect to that number.

But I do not want to sidetrack us here. For me, the goal is to say it enough that when you are not saying it, like an earworm, it is saying itself in your mind.

I once met a Buddhist monk who told a story about how he stayed spiritually aligned during a car accident. When I asked him how he had the presence of mind to stay spiritually aligned, he gave an answer that gets to the heart of what we are doing here. He said, "My mind was not involved; my spiritual practice is such that my response was automatic." He said it just began to flow from him.

This is what we are achieving with our practice: a natural, free-flowing sense of spiritual connection that is more prominent, intimate, and profound than anything else that is happening at the moment, regardless of whether we are at home or on the job.

Sensei Subira: That is breathtaking! I love that! Now, let us get back to that eclectic flexible practice you mentioned earlier. Tell us more about that and why you think that is important?

Reverend Kelli: Great! And this is also a part of mindset. The bottom line is that you only want to do what works. You have to give yourself time to try whatever it is, to get comfortable with it, and to imbue it with faith. You have to give yourself time to surrender resistance to the process. Still, at a certain point, you may sense that a given practice just is not adding to your sense of spiritual connection.

Every spiritual practice that exists came into being because someone was guided by Spirit to invent it.

At that point, it is time to tweak or choose something different. The same is true even if you have used a technique for years and it worked in the past but is not working now. The same is true if the technique worked for everyone else you know but is not working for you. This is your dream, your world, your projection, your co-creation. What you choose has to work for you at the time you are choosing it.

Remember, that which drew you closer to your Divine Self before may not be that which draws you closer to your Divine Self now. You want to accumulate energy through repetition, but you do not want to operate from a sense of habit. Each practice and each encounter with Spirit should be fresh and authentic. You should feel it. If you cannot, it is time for a change.

Sensei Subira: That is interesting. So, how would you sum that up?

Reverend Kelli: It is about effectiveness, not tradition. Do what works for you. Dump what does not, even if you read it here. Effectiveness is the goal. Connection is the goal. This requires that we be flexible, open to borrowing from other traditions, and even open to using Spirit's guidance to invent practices that are effective for us. Because of the connection between religion and culture people may be hesitant and reluctant to engage in "religious appropriation." This is a legitimate concern. All things are to be undertaken with the energy of honor and respect. Yet, know that every inspired method of connecting with God is an aspect of the kingdom of God that belongs to all. Would a true religion wish any believer to be deprived of using a tool that effectively connects that believer to Spirit? And, if there were such an objection, would that objection originate from God or man? Remember, every spiritual practice that exists came into being because someone was guided by Spirit to invent it.

If a practice supports you in feeling your connection with God, give yourself permission to use it.

Sensei Subira: Wow!

Reverend Kelli: What I think of is the word "freedom." I feel free and I advocate that others feel free to craft their own relationship with God and to honor that relationship with methods of connection that are decided upon by them and God, regardless of whether anyone else authorizes, approves, or agrees with the methods used.

Sensei Subira: How did you come to this realization?

Reverend Kelli: I believe the realization was gradual. It probably came from having Attention Deficit Disorder (ADD). I needed non-traditional or new ways of doing things. I would get bored easily and get distracted by my boredom. The tedium of repeatedly doing a specific practice would outweigh its benefit. In other words, the tedium would give rise to resistance that would become an obstacle to connection. This all led to a lot of spiritual exploration and invention. Until, over time I was so aware of my connection it was pretty easy for me to feel it at a deep level of intensity, no matter what process I used. Still, I just really love this stuff. I love mixing and matching, exploring, tweaking! Trying something new is amplifying for me because I am predisposed to appreciate newness.

This mindset is especially useful on the job. Of course, many of us have jobs that are predictable and constant over time. A job like this lends itself to adopting a group of practices and applying them every day. Others, however, have jobs in very dynamic environments, where the daily routine is constantly shifting. Either way, I find that for purposes of maintaining a fresh and authentic connection with Spirit it is supportive to have a wide variety of options, a deep spiritual bench if you are into sports, a big playbook, or as will be discussed later, a huge toolbox.

*Repeat and Believe a Single Truth,
See with a Single Eye, and Open to
Multifaceted Forms of Connection.*

Chapter

If You Build It, God WILL Come:
Building Your Spiritual Toolkit

Heroes take journeys, confront dragons, and discover the treasure of their true selves.

~ Carol Pearson ~

The self-explorer, whether he wants to or not, becomes an explorer of everything else.

~ Elias Canetti ~

We have to figure out which way to go by moving along, by being curious, by experimenting. Most of all, we need to trust our instincts and our innate sense of direction.

~ Lewis Richmond ~

The name of this game is fun and adventure! If you have fun with your practice, you will do it, and doing it is key! In this chapter and this book, I want to do more than just support you in unleashing your Divine Self on the job; I want to support you in sizzling with excitement and delight, in absolutely falling in love with your Divinity and your practice. Experiencing your Divinity is the best way to fall in love. It is energizing, invigorating, and exciting. It will fill you with zeal in a way you have never been filled before. This is what we are up to in the next set of questions and answers.

This is your spiritual toolkit and you get to take charge of it!

I will offer a *Master Tool* called, the *Connection Portal,* and a buffet of other tools for you to choose from when designing your toolkit. You will choose what you think will work for you, and you will own your results. If you try something and it is not a good fit, try something else. Relax and be free. This is your spiritual toolkit and you get to take charge of it!

Building the toolkit yourself is the best way to avoid triggering resistance, and to ensure the creation of a toolkit customized perfectly to fit your Divine Self and your life on the job. I will be with you every step of the way. I will offer suggestions and techniques for ferreting out the types of tools that may be valuable to you. I will tell you what has worked for me.

Here is the one thing that I ask of you, if you discover or invent an effective new practice or tool, tell me about it! Join our group on Facebook[8] and share your creations, manifestations, and experiences.

Remember, the tools you choose for this on-the-job toolkit probably will need to be a little different than the tools you use at home or in other contexts. I will suggest tools that allow you to quickly, or even automatically, shift into spiritual connection without taking significant time away from your job. Also, when you are deciding which tools will work for you, you will want to choose tools you can use while working on your job. If your job requires the use of your hands, you will need hands-free tools. If your job requires you to be on the phone or the computer, your tools will need to be tools you can use while being on the phone or computer. Be sure to weigh these kinds of considerations when customizing your toolkit.

Now let us dive in!

Sensei Subira: Reverend Kelli I know that right up front you wanted to tell the readers about something fundamental.

Reverend Kelli: That is right, this is foundational, and I want it to be understood at the outset.

Sensei Subira: I am excited! What is it?

Reverend Kelli: It is the *Master Tool*, Sensei, the *Connection Portal*.

Sensei Subira: The *Connection Portal!* I like the sound of that! How does it work?

Reverend Kelli: I am glad you asked! First, like all the tools I offer, it is to be tailored to the individual preferences of the person using it. The goal of the *Connection Portal* is a turbo-charged connection. It is designed to get you to God in 22 seconds or less, and when you use it regularly and get good at it, you can make that connection virtually instantaneously. You have heard of the 30-second elevator pitch. Well, with this tool, you are going to get yourself to God before the pitch finishes, with a full 8 seconds to spare.

The *Connection Portal* begins with the first step: *Intention*. Craft a short statement in your own words and your own voice that expresses your intention to connect with the God of *your* understanding. Speak in the way you normally would, not in a stilted or formal fashion. When you speak it, it should feel real for you. It should be a statement that you feel expresses your sincere and authentic desire to connect with your God. Spend the time, in the beginning, to make it feel good because you will work with this intention and with the *Connection Portal* as a precursor to most of the practices offered here. Your intention statement will signal God that you desire to experience conscious awareness of your Divine connection.

Next, is the *Reality Reversal*. This is an act, sound, movement, vision, whatever works best for you. You decide. The Reality Reversal is a reminder you choose so that you remember that God is the only true reality. It affirms that anything you are experiencing that does not align with God has no reality

> *Experience yourself as one with the flow of Spirit.*

and no power. In this step, you release the so-called real world. This step is meant to be an interrupter, so choose something that feels a bit jarring but can still be done in the presence of other people if need be. My Reality Reversal is putting my hands in my prayer position, rubbing them together, blowing into them like I am warming them up, rolling my head back, and with my head back, interlacing my fingers and bringing my hands up toward the sky. Then, I slowly lower my arms with a deep breath and a sigh. The order on it may change depending on how I feel at the moment. You do not need to do all of that. One movement, or sound or vision, or whatever you choose is fine. I have ADD so I prefer to do several acts to break the reality trance that is the world. My process brings me into a new space. The movements also are physically empowering and energizing. As always, the key is to use movements or visions or sounds that work for you, not necessarily the ones that work for me.

The third step is *Peace*. This step is easy. It is the pause where you allow yourself to feel the presence of God within and all around you, the pulse of God beating your heart, and the flow of God running through your veins. With the eyes open, inhale; let them close on the exhale. Repeat three times or as necessary until you feel the presence of stillness.

The last step is *Alignment*. See yourself as a straight line, a line where God enters through the top of your head and flows to the earth from the bottom of your feet. See, feel, and imagine this flow becoming so intense that it is like standing in a waterfall. Now, surrender, let go of boundaries (these boundaries represent resistance, all the places you have said no to Spirit, all that you would not allow God to do through you), let yourself be boundaryless and porous so the water of God flows in and out of you freely. Experience yourself as one with the flow of Spirit.

Become the *Connection Portal*!

Sensei Subira: It sounds like a great process. It seems like it will take longer than 22 seconds though.

How does this get me to God in 22 seconds?

Reverend Kelli: Sensei, you know what I am going to say! Practice! Practice! Practice! Practice is the name of the game. Like anything. Like a magic trick. It is slow and clunky in the beginning, but with practice, it works like magic. I would liken it to roller skating or ice skating. In the beginning, it is slow rolling, but with practice, you will be racing around the rink like it is nothing.

These steps should be used together, at first. With practice, each will become a cue that triggers the other. In other words, they will energetically begin to reinforce each other, calling one another to mind, priming you to connect, such that the doing of one will be like the doing of them all. When that happens, you will have multiple instant techniques to transport yourself to God. Of course, you are not going anywhere, you are simply shifting your awareness into a sense of connection with the truth of the Presence of Spirit, in, as, all around, and through you.

Sensei Subira: Uhm! Uhm! Uhm! I am on this! The *Connection Portal*, Yes! What else do you have for us, Reverend Kelli?

Reverend Kelli: Plenty! But I want to make sure folks master the *Connection Portal*. Wherever I talk about connecting with Spirit, I am referencing the use of this tool, in whatever way the person may have adapted it for themselves. Virtually every tool and principle discussed here calls upon folks to connect with God first, so mastering a technique to do that is paramount.

Sensei Subira: I get that this is important. Okay, while folks are digesting that process, let us switch gears for a bit. I would like to go to the flipside. Let us talk about some things that do not help. Are there any tools or resources you think are outdated or obsolete?

Reverend Kelli: Dated or not, if a tool is effective and supportive, there is no reason not to use it. After all, some of our Sacred Texts are ancient. One perspective that I find not useful, or outdated if you prefer, is the view that Sacred Texts and church are the *only* mechanisms for understanding, experiencing, and sharing God.

Sensei Subira: That is interesting and unexpected! Are you of the opinion that these modes of experiencing Spirit are less effective or influential than they once were?

Reverend Kelli: It is not that their influence is dwindling. They are still powerful and important. People are still becoming inspired by reading Sacred Text and attending church. But, today, when folks go to church, they are not just getting God and fellowship; they are getting so much more: an entire social and, in some cases, social media and technological experience. Churches stream. They have websites, podcasts, online services, donate buttons, bigger and bigger choirs, even liturgical dance. The reading of Sacred Text is an aspect of the whole production. Churches are in a world where multisensory experience is sought after. They must produce an experience that competes with a fantastic world of technology that sings siren songs, not right outside the church doors, but right inside the pocket or purse of their parishioners.

Have I connected with Spirit at church? Sure, I have! I have also connected with Spirit many times outside of a church, with and without the use of Sacred Text.

What works and what does not work has to do with where the individual is in consciousness.

Sensei Subira: So, church and Sacred Text are a way of connecting but not the only way?

Reverend Kelli: Exactly! We can connect with our inner core and experience who and what God is, in a variety of other ways, especially when connecting on the job.

I think it is important to have a spiritual practice that incorporates every experience I have and reveals to me how that experience fits into the puzzle of who I am in God. When it comes to experiencing my Divine Self on the job, I need a spiritual practice that supports the processing of life experiences as those experiences occur, no matter where I am.

Sensei Subira: What about tools? Are there any everyday spiritual tools that you find challenging?

Reverend Kelli: I am hesitant to name those because what I find challenging may be perfect for someone else. Plus, what works and what does not work has to do with where the individual is in consciousness.

Sensei Subira: Where the individual is in consciousness? How does that impact things?

Reverend Kelli: Well, I will just use myself as an example. I have seen myself evolve in the depth of my faith. The more faith I have in general, and the more faith I have in the specific tool, the better things work. Faith makes tools more effective. Faith is a function of consciousness. Doubt and resistance interfere with and dilute the effect of a tool. You may remember that Jesus, though a renowned healer who healed the sick throughout the New Testament and was prophesied about in the Old (Isaiah 35:5-6; Matthew 14:33; John 11:47; John 9:1; John 6:19; John 2:1; Matthew 12:22; John 11:43-44), is reported to have had difficulty healing in his hometown (Mark 6:1-5; Matthew 13:54-58). Why . . . because the people of his hometown had little faith in him. They knew him as Mary's son, as Joseph the carpenter's son, and their lack of faith in Jesus as an intercessor weakened their ability to activate the healing power within them.

As I have evolved, the tools that I have had success with have changed significantly. I once was able to sit and meditate for only a short period before becoming distracted. I sincerely wanted to meditate, but it was torture, in part because I experience ADD. I kept trying though! I discovered I could do walking and writing meditations. People with ADD have the gift of hyper-focus and that gift helped me. I realized that when I am intensely interested in an activity, that activity becomes like a meditation for me. So, I began to do activities with a meditative intention. I began to pay attention to what was revealed and healed through it. Now, I have become good at going within quickly and deeply. The funny thing I noticed is that now sitting meditations are no problem for me. I love them. I do not always make time for them, but I love them.

Now *tapping*, also known as, *Emotional Freedom Technique* or *EFT*, is a fantastic tool and could be a powerful part of an on-the-job toolkit. There are plenty of online resources and videos that explain exactly how the process works. It is a great way to release stuck energy and transcend negative beliefs, behaviors, and circumstances. Yet, while it is great, tapping is challenging for me. I love the idea of tapping. People I love and respect have experienced tremendous transformation through tapping. I have practiced tapping many times in many ways. While tapping is not a tool that has been successful for me, my experience does not diminish tapping's value as a tool. I have recommended tapping for coaching clients, and I recommend that readers explore it as a possible tool for their toolkit.

Sensei Subira: I understand your point that readers may still benefit from tapping despite your experience, but I am curious. I am familiar with tapping, and I wonder what it is about it that does not work for you. Is there something specific?

Reverend Kelli: There is! I attribute it to a quote that has always stuck in my mind. I think it may have been said by Myrtle Fillmore, one of the founders of the Unity Movement. The quote is, "Never say anything you do not want to be true."

Tapping uses set-up statements that set the stage for the issue to be addressed by having you describe the existing undesirable condition. Words have power!

Tools only work if you work them.

I experience a lot of resistance when I practice tapping because I am caught up in the set-up statements. My resistance is that describing the condition for me feels like reinforcing the condition. Also, I am a little challenged when it comes to coordinating my taps with my statements.

So, as you can see, my difficulties with the tapping tool are personal. Our experience with a tool will be unique to us. The very tool that draws one person directly into the heart of their God Self may have zero impact on another person.

Sensei Subira: Is there anything ubiquitous that is true or should be true about all the tools in the toolbox for spirituality on the job?

Reverend Kelli: What is universally true about these tools and processes, and all tools and processes, is that to be effective, they must be used. Tools only work if you work them.

Hermes Trismegistus is quoted in the *Kybalion* as saying: "The possession of knowledge unless accompanied by a manifestation and expression in action, is like the hoarding of precious metals: a vain and foolish thing. Knowledge, like wealth, is intended for use."[9]

So, these tools and processes are activations. They are a way of activating, preserving, and locking in the knowledge gained. You must *use it or lose it*.

Sensei Subira: So, Reverend Kelli, what other tools can we put in our on-the-job toolkit?

Reverend Kelli: Here are some of my favorite things. Now, remember, the key is that these are things that get me pumped up and keep me connected to Spirit. Each person needs to explore what does that for them.

The key to an on-the-job toolkit is to identify portable tools.

An *altar* is a great tool for transforming the energy in a physical space. Depending on how long I expect to be stationed in one place, I sometimes create a *mini altar* on my desk. My goal is not to announce my altar to others or to make anyone around me take notice or be uncomfortable. My goal is to manage the energy in my environment. There are tons of books on altar making. Here is my take. My altar consists of objects that add positive energy to my environment. This positive energy offsets the impact that other people and situations have on me. To the eye of an onlooker, my altar looks benign and insignificant. There is a picture of my son, a precious stone, a positive quote, and sticky notes upon which I write inspirations from Spirit, as I experience them. There is also lavender scented, spray-on natural hand sanitizer that I use to smudge my space.[10]

Sensei Subira: Reverend Kelli, will you explain what you mean by smudging for anyone who is not familiar with it?

Reverend Kelli: *Smudging* is a sacred practice commonly used in Native American ceremonies and the ceremonies of other traditional religions. It is used to cleanse the mental, emotional, and spiritual body, and the physical space. While smudging is typically done using smoke from setting fire to plants like Sage, Cedar, Sweetgrass, and Palo Santo (holy wood), in my experience, any substance that dissipates negativity can be used, and many people smudge using liquid sprays or clear energy by diffusing essential oils. On the job, my lavender hand sanitizer is a subtle and effective method. This is the kind of improvising I encourage. I hope people will experiment.

I find that lavender helps me to reduce stress and its lingering smell keeps me feeling positive and reminds me of my positive prayer or intention. For more information on smudging, I encourage people to look online where there is an abundance of information available. But I do want to make this last point. While burning or spraying, whatever negativity dissipater is selected, a prayer, declaration, or intention statement should be spoken (or mentally spoken). Again, people ought to select words that feel authentic to them. Whatever language is used should express the sentiment that all energy in the space and your body is transformed, that negative energy is cleansed and becomes positive, and that positive energy is elevated, amplified, and expanded.

Sensei Subira: I love smudging!

Reverend Kelli: Me too! Now, let me tell folks about a few other tools I use.

Sensei Subira: Go ahead.

Reverend Kelli: Another tool I use is *sound*. I use the Audible application for books and vibratory frequency recordings. I use my phone's podcast app to listen to podcasts. I have my favorite sermons on my Dropbox app, and I listen to those. I have recordings of live events that spiritually inspire me, like recordings of me and others singing sacred chants. I have a digital music subscription, and I listen to music that inspires me. This is different than what I have at home where I use some of these same things and may incorporate gongs, singing bowls, rattles, bells, and other instruments and toning tools.

> *The body needs to experience the energy of life flowing through it.*

I like *scriptural and meditation apps*. During a project, I also read a huge number of spiritual and inspirational quotes, as I subscribe to several lists that send out daily or weekly inspirations, like Daily-Bible-Verse.org, Daily Quotes from Abraham-Hicks and, of course, I check out whatever is being offered by spiritual mentors and teachers like Mama Iyanla (Reverend Doctor Iyanla Vanzant) and Brother Ishmael Tetteh.

Deep breathing is another great tool that can be used on the job. I would activate the *Peace* step in the *Connection Portal* process. But there are a lot of breathing exercises out there. Folks need to adopt a method that works for them. Breathing exercises are very valuable in combating physical symptoms that throw us out of alignment, such as the amygdala hijack (when the fear center of our brain hijacks rational thinking and triggers an extreme stress response), and adrenal fatigue (when stressors have overstimulated the adrenal glands). But one way for folks to support themselves on the job or at home is to make sure they are breathing properly. When breathing in, the belly should expand. When breathing out, the belly should contract.

Sensei Subira: Breathing is so important! As a martial artist, I know exactly how critical it is.

Reverend Kelli: That's right, and breathing can be coupled with a brief meditation or stilling of the mind, an intention statement, or a declaration.

Reverend Kelli: I want to mention four other tools: *Exercise, Creativity, Acceptance,* and *Prayer*. Each of these is exceptional in the workplace. *Exercise* may seem like more of a stress reliever, but the body is often the drag, the aspect of being that is out of alignment. The body needs to experience the energy of life flowing through it.

When the body does not get what it needs (which it often does not during those hours on the job), it can become a resting place for dead, negative, and stagnant energies. These energies themselves become a type of resistance that operates like static and can interfere with the depth of our awareness of Divine Presence. These energies need to be cleared and released, as soon as possible. Stretching, bending over to touch the toes, standing on tiptoes and stretching the entire body upward, twisting the back, twisting the waist, rolling the neck, and walking, are all ways of infusing the body with energy by subtly exercising at work. Exercise is an extraordinary clearing mechanism!

Creativity is next. Creativity is among my favorite tools because it builds on itself and is usually accompanied by the added benefit of inspiration. Creativity and inspiration amplify each other. Activities like doodling, making up songs, combing our hair, and rearranging our workspace all activate Creativity. As we continue indulging in creative acts, even small ones, more Creativity is activated. Creativity gives birth to inspiration, and inspiration to more Creativity. Like the snake consuming itself, Creativity feeds on itself inexhaustibly. Inspiration and Creativity, once stirred up, can be applied to work on the job. As with all tools, Creativity works best when it is preceded by the use of the *Connection Portal.*

Sensei Subira: What about Acceptance and Prayer?

Reverend Kelli: *Acceptance* is one of the most powerful tools available at work or home. I call it a tool because I think of it as a tool, and I want people to start thinking of Acceptance and Creativity, and other energies as tools that can be cultivated, activated, and applied to a situation. Energies are more than just feelings that randomly come upon us. We can choose them and use them. Acceptance frees our energy and frees us from resistance. With Acceptance, instead of wasting energy fighting against things, we can conserve and channel energy, move forward, and address and cope with situations.

There is a prayer popularized by members of the Alcoholics Anonymous program called the Serenity Prayer. It can be a powerful support in activating the energy of Acceptance. Written by Reinhold Niebuhr, there are numerous versions of the prayer; below is a popularized abbreviated form.[11]

Serenity Prayer

God, grant me the serenity to accept the things I cannot change,

the courage to change the things I can,

and the wisdom to know the difference.

Amen.

Sensei Subira: So, to use the tool of Acceptance, do people just pray this prayer?

Reverend Kelli: No, no. It begins with the *Connection Portal.* Connect with Spirit. Reflect positively on the situation being accepted. Feel that all is well with the situation. Choose *Acceptance* and make a declaration of Acceptance, such as: "At the depths of my being, I accept the company's decision to promote Joe. I release all resistance to Joe's promotion and all attachment to having the promotion for myself. May my acceptance deepen, and my attachment and resistance weaken with each recitation of the Serenity Prayer."

Sensei Subira: These other steps lay a foundation then?

Reverend Kelli: Yes, and this same kind of foundation can be used to call forth whatever energetic tool we need. *Courage! Persistence! Inner Authority! Wisdom! Strength! Detachment!* Whatever we need is available to us and can be called forth from the Divine Realms.

Sensei Subira: And, after the foundation is laid, that is where Prayer comes in?

Reverend Kelli: Yes, a formal *prayer* can be attached at that point. This foundation is an abbreviated form of a process I teach called *Energetic Programming*.

As you know, Sensei, it is all *Prayer*: all our thoughts, all we hold in mind, all that we say. So, the laying of the foundation also is Prayer in a sense. We can pray in our own words. We can pray a prayer written by another or we can use passages of Sacred Text as a Prayer. In this way, the text also is a tool.

Sensei Subira: Are there any passages that make particularly good Prayer tools?

Reverend Kelli: There are plenty!

But first, I should acknowledge that I do not use formal Prayer as a regular tool in my toolkit. I Pray often and my Prayers are usually the Prayers of my heart, using my own words because they feel more authentic for me, and they activate my faith.

There is a benefit to praying with Sacred Text! Sacred Text has been used repeatedly by so many for so long, and it is infused with so much energy, that when you use it to pray, you have an energetic head start. The Prayer is imprinted with power, and when you speak it, you are activating a template, kindling a universal memory, and leapfrogging over your

> *Prayer energizes outcomes that align with the energy of the Prayer, gradually transitioning those outcomes from the realm of the possible to the realm of the actual.*

angst and resistance. The two Psalms below have been used through the generations for Prayer support.

Psalms 121: 1-2

I lift my eyes to the hills. From where will my help come? My help comes from the Lord, who made heaven and earth.

Psalm 23

The Lord is my shepherd; I shall not want
He maketh me to lie down in green pastures;
He leadeth me beside the still waters.
He restoreth my soul; He leadeth me in the paths of
righteousness for His name's sake.
Yea, though I walk through the valley of the
Shadow of death, I will fear no evil; for Thou art with me;
Thy rod and Thy staff they comfort me.
Thou preparest a table before me in the presence of mine enemies;
Thou anointest my head with oil; my cup runneth over.
Surely goodness and mercy shall follow me all the days of my life;
And I will dwell in the house of the Lord forever.

Reverend Kelli: The Psalms are prayed in many different spiritual traditions and their effectiveness is widely recognized.

Sensei Subira: They are!

Sensei Subira: Listen, Reverend Kelli, I am curious; tell us more about the Energetic Programming process you mentioned earlier?

Reverend Kelli: Okay, great! The process involves purifying energy and layering intentions. I will give a usable summary here to let folks get a start.

Here is how it works. Outcomes, both desirable and undesirable, exist in the realm of possibility. Prayer energizes outcomes that align with the energy of the Prayer, gradually transitioning those outcomes from the realm of the possible to the realm of the actual.

The more faith we have in the manifestation of our Prayer, the more energized it is, and the more readily it manifests the outcomes with which it aligns.

Sensei Subira: Is there a way for people to build more faith so their Prayers are more energizing?

Reverend Kelli: A mentor of mine, Reverend Sylvia Sumter, often taught that we already have all the faith we are ever going to have. I think what she meant by that is that faith is not something we get more of, it is something we awaken and direct! In *Energetic Programming,* this act of awakening and directing is called, *Establishing the Proofs*. It is a simple process of remembering and documenting God's demonstrated willingness to answer prayers and be a force for good in our lives. I recommend that people establish a list of proofs that awaken within them a feeling tone of faith. After connecting with Spirit and before Praying, direct attention to this list of proofs and announce it repeatedly until the feeling of faith flows.

Sensei Subira: So, *Establishing the Proofs* is a faith directing and awakening step that folks need to take ahead of the other parts of the process?

Reverend Kelli: Yes, it is one of the first preparatory steps. And it sounds like this:

I call upon Mother, Father, God Almighty, the same God who _____ (add proof statements such as, healed my mother when she was hospitalized, mended my broken heart when my husband and I divorced, empowered me to graduate from law school, inspired me to deliver talks around the country, manifested money for me when I was unemployed, etc.)

Sensei Subira: The proof statements ultimately will become a part of the prayer itself?

Reverend Kelli: Yes, exactly, these steps will come together in a master prayer that we implant, but we will get to that.

A corrupted prayer may yield a corrupt outcome.

Sensei Subira: Okay, tell us more!

Reverend Kelli: When fear and worldly desires vibrate within a prayer, which is most of the time if we have not taken conscious steps to cleanse it, then the vibratory frequency of the prayer is compromised.

As prayer energizes an outcome aligned with its vibration, a corrupted prayer may yield a corrupt outcome.

James 4:3-4 says we do not receive because we ask amiss. Corrupted prayers ask amiss. The next step in *Energetic Programming, Purifying the Prayer,* is a way of cleaning up the asking process.

Fears and worldly desires have no substance. They may seem true in the physical sense; still, they are not a part of the immutable and eternal Truth of Spirit. They are not True with a capital T. They hide Truth within them if we are willing to take the time to interview and dissect them. So, say, for example, I am constructing a prayer for a promotion and I find underlying my prayer worldly energies, a desire for status, greed, and jealousy, and fear of failure and lack. My next step would be to go into these energies and get to their core. If I keep digging and discover the Truth, I discover I do not want status. I want the power to be kind and good. I am not greedy. I desire to experience the freedom of God's abundance. I am not jealous.

> *The energy of the Divine is always operating to expand the fruits of the Spirit.*

I see the Divinity in another, and I desire to express Divinity within myself. I am not afraid of failure or lack. Again, I long to express my Divinity and experience God's abundance. This process of stripping away the false and anchoring the Truth is the process of Purifying the Prayer. Instead of a prayer corrupted by fear and worldly desires, what I will be left with is a prayer whose fulfillment will expand the fruits of the Spirit: love, joy, peace, patience, kindness, goodness, faithfulness, gentleness, self-control, and other Divine energies (Galatians 5:22-23). The energy of the Divine is always operating to expand the fruits of the Spirit.

Thus, when the fulfillment of a Prayer leads to the expansion of the fruits of the Spirit, the Prayer naturally aligns with what Spirit is already about the business of doing. Everything is easy, natural, and non-resistant. This is what we want! Step two sounds like this:

God, I ask you to demonstrate the fruits of the Spirit through me now. Demonstrate _____ (fill in the appropriate fruit, for example, abundance) through me now by manifesting the Divinely perfect fulfillment of this prayer for a new and more responsible position.

Sensei Subira: Got it! What is step three?

Reverend Kelli: Step three has two parts: *Purifying the Vessel* and *Fueling the Prayer*. Not only do we need to cleanse the Prayer of worldly energies and fears, but we also need to cleanse ourselves, since we are the ones who will be praying the Prayer. Jesus said if we come to the altar and remember that we are not at peace with our brother, we are to go and make peace, then return. And, since we are to love our brother as ourselves, I believe that directive also is a directive to be at peace with ourselves, before praying at the altar. At any given moment, we have all sorts of disquieting thoughts, beliefs, and experiences occupying our energetic field.

At any given moment, we have all sorts of disquieting thoughts, beliefs, and experiences occupying our energetic field.

To purify ourselves before we pray, we need to call forth and become conscious of any dissipating and disruptive energies, as such energies could shut down channels through which our Prayer might be answered.

In this step, we call forth pain, hate, anger, upset, jealousy, grief, fear, antagonism. We call forth any obstructionist energies, and from a place of connection to Spirit, we call in Divine Transmuting Energy. The goal here is to transmute obstructions and fuel the manifestation of the Prayer. After it is complete, we announce that it is done. Purifying the vessel and fueling the Prayer sounds like this:

Love and healing energy have transmuted all pain from the breakup with Joe. The energy from this experience, pure love energy, now fuels the full manifestation of my prayer.

Sensei Subira: What if we have a lot of obstructionist energy? Can we have a lot of statements? Or do we boil all the events down into one statement?

Reverend Kelli: Either way is fine. If there are a lot of different types of obstructionist energy, multiple statements are probably the way to go. Otherwise, if the energies are related, or related to one upset, one general statement is possible. That is fine.

Sensei Subira: What is the next step?

Reverend Kelli: The next step is *Raising the Vibration*. In this step, you read Sacred Text or other enlightened writings, listen to high vibrational music, burn frankincense or burn or spray other scents that call you into the presence, engage in running, painting, or another spiritually engrossing activity, or visit beautiful or natural places where you can become one with the sacred.

The purpose of this step is to amplify your state of consciousness before implanting the Prayer. Up to this point, the focus has been on becoming clear and praying a clear Prayer. This step is about further amplifying the energy of the Prayer by amplifying your energy before you pray it, implant it onto an object, a repeating event, or a blessing done for another.

Sensei Subira: Implant? That is an interesting word. How do you implant the Prayer?

Reverend Kelli: After the proofs have been established (the same set of proofs can be used every time the process is performed), the prayer has been purified, and the method for raising the vibration determined, the next decision is to determine how to implant the Prayer.

Energetic Programming requires a lot of effort and energy. It results in a Prayer with a super high vibration that will be prayed from a super high vibratory state. The purpose of implanting the Prayer is to keep the high energy alive and keep the Prayer going.

Sensei Subira: To preserve it?

Reverend Kelli: Yes! As humans, we vary, and our vibration changes. We waiver! We doubt! We resist! Today when we pray a Prayer that Prayer might vibrate at 150, tomorrow it may be at 50 (I am using numbers to illustrate the point, not to suggest that vibration is numerically quantifiable). The purpose of *Energetic Programming* is to create a Prayer that vibrates at 1000 and holds that vibration. Once that Prayer is created, we want to lock in the energy and ensure it does not dissipate.

We lock it in by hooking it to a repeating circumstance.

Sensei Subira: Like the example, you showed us with the Serenity Prayer when you said: "May my acceptance deepen, and my attachment and resistance weaken with each recitation of the Serenity Prayer."

Reverend Kelli: You are 100% correct, that is it! We can put a repeating hook on any Prayer but putting it on a Prayer that already has a high vibratory frequency is the difference between putting a turbocharged engine in a go-cart and putting one in a Ferrari. The Ferrari is already built to perform!

Sensei Subira: So, with *Energetic Programming,* we are producing Ferrari Prayers!

Reverend Kelli: Believe it!

> *Prayers can be implanted on a tool like EDMAM or on something as common as a rock or a computer keyboard that sits on a desk and is seen and touched regularly.*

Now let me conclude our discussion of *Energetic Programming* by giving people a few sample implant statements and talking about why this process is so useful for the on-the-job toolkit.

I also do implants on prayer devices. I call the device an EDMAM, which stands for Enhancement Device for Manifestation and Mindfulness. I make them out of copper wire, (which conducts energy) and crystals or semiprecious stones like amethyst. I consecrate or bless the EDMAM to support mindfulness and the manifestation of my Prayers. Then, whenever I interact with the EDMAM I am reinforcing my Prayer. Prayers can be implanted on a tool like EDMAM or on something as common as a rock or a computer keyboard that sits on a desk and is seen and touched regularly.

They can also be implanted on something that naturally repeats, like the beating of a heart or the exhalation and inhalation of breath. A third way to do an implant is to release any thought of the Prayer or its manifestation. You do a good deed and then consecrate the positive energy that flows from that good deed to fuel the fulfillment of your Prayer. This third method is particularly powerful when you are praying to enhance a personal quality like wisdom or confidence, or even competence.

> *Energetic Programming allows us to layer intentions.*

Sensei Subira: I can see there is so much more to *Energetic Programming*. Are you still offering this course in case folks want to learn more?

Reverend Kelli: I have not offered it in a bit, but I may write a separate book that covers the process in detail, and it may even come with an EDMAM!

Sensei Subira: Keep me posted on that, Reverend Kelli! Now, let us get back to those implant statements.

Reverend Kelli: Alright! Here we go with the examples!

Implant 1. I declare and command that the energy of this prayer will continue to vibrate in and through this keyboard, expanding each time I touch, see, or handle the keyboard, and pulling forth the full manifestation of this prayer from unseen to seen!

Implant 2. I declare and command that with each beat of my heart the energy of this prayer again will be sent out into the Universe to go forth and accomplish that which it is sent forth to do.

Implant 3. I declare and command that the energy of this prayer is now sealed so that it will and may only expand and multiply 10-fold with each blessing I bestow on Joe Smith and each blessing that flows from that blessing, on and on until every person is blessed by this prayer.

Just in case it is not obvious how all of this connects to the on-the-job toolkit Energetic Programming allows us to layer intentions.

By implanting Prayers on objects and more or less having Prayer energy active in the workspace, having Prayers active in the body, and actively connecting with Spirit at work and praying Prayers, stating intentions, and making declarations, there is a multi-layered activation of Divine Energy in play.

Sensei Subira: Powerful!

Reverend Kelli: *Energetic Programming* is a kind of hybrid tool. A lot of the preparatory work can be done before arriving on the job, and then the rest can be done on the job, and the benefits enjoyed on the job.

Sensei Subira: Are there any other hybrid tools like that?

Reverend Kelli: The *living* aspect to my toolkit is a bit of a hybrid, in that I can access it at home or on the job. My High Council is what I am referring to. I have an informal group of people that I can reach out to for support. These are people I can trust to support me from the place of their Divinity, not from fear or an attachment to material concepts like status, greed, jealousy, and lust for power. They are people who will intercede for me when I feel challenged and detached from Spirit or overwhelmed with emotions and unable to establish a clear connection. They are people who will coach me, hold me accountable, pray with me, speak Truth to me, and generally support me in shifting. They are people who will quickly respond to my call or text. You are one of those people, Sensei!

Sensei Subira: As you are for me, Sis! As you are for me.

Now, Reverend Kelli, what about tools that folks can use outside of their job that will support them on the job?

Reverend Kelli: Coaching is by far one of the most influential tools that I have witnessed and participated in people using successfully to elevate their job experience. Life experiences offer learning and opportunities for evolution. You want to take the experience, play it back in slow-motion, and process it. Processing means ferreting out what the experience has to offer in terms of growth. You can do it on your own, and should, and you also can do it with the support of a coach whose job it is to ground the Truth and hold space for you. Coaching provides an opportunity to disrupt harmful patterns, dissect experiences, learn and recognize the operation of spiritual principles, and test new behaviors and beliefs. I have seen coaching shift entire career trajectories. And, in a sense, my career trajectory shifted entirely when I attended the Inner Visions Institute for Spiritual Development, where I was coached and learned to coach.

Also, it is not a tool per se, but the spiritual work you do away from the job also has an impact on the job. This especially pays off if it is spiritual work related to your significant other and your family. Because no matter how much you attempt to separate the job from home, the important things happening at home likely impact your experience on the job (and vice versa). Family relationships imprint on us. Our family imprint colors the way we behave in any organization. The impact is more profound when the structural dynamics of the organization closely mirror the dynamics of our family.

The last technique, a technique we have discussed in other chapters, is identifying and doing True Work! Doing True Work deepens spiritual connection and is so deeply satisfying it heals other hurts in our lives, both on the job and at home. It allows us to see our role in life more clearly and it reprioritizes our concerns so that petty things fade into the background, and all that is not of God becomes petty.

Sensei Subira: Wow! This has been a delicious buffet of tools! Are there any others or any final thoughts on the creation of the on-the-job toolkit that you want us to know?

Reverend Kelli: I hope you get the bottom-line message that everything can become a tool.

Things become tools by your intention to use them to enhance your spiritual practice.

Everything can become a tool. Things become tools by your intention to use them to enhance your spiritual practice.

Any energy can be called in, any person can become an ally (i.e. *I declare and intend that when I speak to Joe today, I will be inspired and encouraged by his words*), any situation can become an opportunity for evolution. By setting an intention for ourselves (not for another, although our intention may involve interacting with another), we can use any situation or person as a mechanism for spiritual growth.

In the morning as you shower and dress to go to work, you ought to bless yourself and lay a foundation for your day on the job. What kind of energy do you need to call in? Call it in! Who is it you need to encounter? Call them forth! Is there anyone or anything or any energy you need to shield yourself from? Activate a white light covering (i.e. *I call upon the white light of God emanating and expanding from within my heart to protect me. I see the external energy of God as a white light surrounding and protecting me. I see the energies uniting in a seal of protection from all that is not in my highest good*). Connection, preparation, foundation, intention, these are the keys to the kingdom! Be creative, customize, and practice, practice, practice!

Tools, the Language We Develop to Connect with Spirit: The More We Have, the More Diverse They Are, the More Assurance We Have That the Conversation Will Continue!

Chapter

8

Design Your Time: The Zen of Where and When

*We must use time creatively, and forever
realize that the time is always ripe to do right.*

~ Martin Luther King, Jr. ~

*Let a man fix his mind on the reality and
having done this, he will transcend time.*

~ Mahabharata ~

*One who is afraid of time becomes a prey of time. But time
itself becomes a prey of that one who is not afraid of it.*

~ Nisargadatta ~

*A butterfly counts not months but
moments, and has time enough.*

~ Rabindranath Tagore ~

Time is. Yet, we do not know what it is or how it works. It is a mystery. And still, like the mystery of God, we can engage and align with it.

Sensei Subira: Is there something that you think people need to know about the experience of time on the job?

Reverend Kelli: People expend an unnecessary amount of time on resistance. They resist being themselves and they resist being who they think the job is causing them to become. In short, too much time is spent on an identity struggle. The resistance I am speaking of is a tension between the subtle yearning to be Divine Self and the external pressure to adopt the mask and become the employee the job wants.

Half of the time when we think we know what the job wants, we are wrong!

I had discerned a ridiculous number of rules for how to succeed at my job. So much to watch out for! It was exhausting and so time-consuming. All that energy, and guess what? Half of the time when we think we know what the job wants, we are wrong!

Then the fallout from our confusion becomes another waste of time.

Aligning with Spirit inspires. Inspiration increases efficiency and efficacy.

Other chapters have discussed masking and resistance at length. So, even though eliminating these energy sucks would be the number one way to increase efficiency and expand available time, here let us talk more specifically about techniques for expanding and contracting time on the job in general.

Sensei Subira: Alright!

Reverend Kelli: First, know that practicing spirituality on the job requires no extra time. Practicing spirituality is in itself a time-management tool. It saves time in a few ways.

Important among these is that it supports full spiritual integration, which allows a spiritual response to become second nature on and off the job. The more you work your practice, the more your practice works. In time, the practice and its fruits blend and begin to appear and show up naturally. Then, the practice simply becomes you, who you are, and how you live. In short, the practice can layer on top of other things that are normally done on the job. It can become an open program running in the foreground of everything you do. Aligning with Spirit inspires. Inspiration increases efficiency and efficacy.

Inspiration is the idea that saves you three working days. It is the energy that transforms a mundane task into a fun mindfulness game. Inspiration generates a reciprocal relationship between the worker and the work so that as the worker is creating the work product, the work product is creating and growing the worker. Inspired work nourishes, expands, grows, and gives birth to newness. Uninspired work drains and depletes.

Sensei Subira: Are there other ways that spiritual alignment impacts time?

Reverend Kelli: Time and Spirit are mystically married.

Practice allows us to move with the support of time so that we have no fight with time.

Sensei Subira: How do people fight with time?

Reverend Kelli: If you are late habitually, you are fighting time! If deadlines are stalking you, you are fighting time! If you feel overwhelmed and overstimulated, you are fighting time! If you feel bored, you are fighting time! I could go on, but I will stop here since the solution is the same.

Sensei Subira: What is that solution?

Reverend Kelli: I call it the Zen of Where and When. Others may call it being here now, being present, or being in the moment. I see it as a two-prong practice.

Sensei Subira: What are the prongs?

Reverend Kelli: Prong 1 is, *be where you are*, and, of course, prong 2 is, *be when you are*.

Sensei Subira: Interesting, tell us more.

Reverend Kelli: Be where you are. If you are on the job, leave home and its stressors behind. If you are at home, do not obsess over problems on the job. Being fully where you are allows you to access all of yourself without dissipation.

The same is true of being when you are. You are on the job working on a project, but instead of being fully present to the project, the project triggers you. It reminds you of your last similar project that went great. You are now daydreaming about what the boss will say and do if this project goes great too. You are in another time, a future time that may or may not come to pass. If you were engaged in the spiritual process of visioning, this would be appropriate. But if you are supposed to be working on the substance of the project this is not a time for you to be in an imagined future.

I chose to use a positive time distraction because being in another time or another place energetically for a happy reason, can be just as dissipating and distracting as being there for an unhappy reason.

Sensei Subira: How can we bring ourselves back if we find ourselves in a different place or time?

The Shift or Return

Reverend Kelli: Perfect question! The *Shift or Return* can be achieved through a simple process of calling back your energy and then using your senses to ground it in the moment. It is less complicated than it sounds, and it is super effective. Let me use an example to show you how it works.

I had a shocking fall a while ago. I was climbing over the gate that kept my dog, Henny, out of the kitchen, and my hands were full of vegetables and a knife. My foot failed to clear the gate, and with my hands full, I had no way of catching my balance. I loudly fell flat on my knees and everything was scattered: the gate, the knife, the vegetables, even wall socket dislodged. I stalled my tears and immediately prayed that all was well with me. My knee was skinned, and it swelled a little, otherwise, I was fine physically, but emotionally I was traumatized. My mind kept cycling to the event of my son coming to check on me and helping me up. At the close of the following day, I realized I had kept the hurt alive. I had been feeding it energy. The pain and shock, horror, and fear of the original fall that I kept reliving had haunted me for reasons that had little to do with the discomfort caused by the residue of physical pain I still felt. I had limped and coddled the injury, told my mother about it, brought it up all the time to anyone who would listen.

- Step 1 - Be present to the awareness that your energy is in another place or time.

- Step 2 - Discover what the payoff is for being in that place or time, or what part of you is stuck there.

- For me, I realized I was stuck because of a fear of suffering a serious injury, and being unable to receive help or compassion or concern from another, awakened in me at the time I hit the ground. And, I had not received enough pampering, concern, or compassion from myself or others since the fall to discharge the fear in the normal course. Intensifying aches and pains were alerting me that I needed to do something, and the something was an emotional release.

- Step 3 - Call your energy back from the time or place you are stuck. Like this, "I call my energy back from the fall. I release the fear of being alone and uncared for, and I release every attachment to the fall." The third part of the statement, "I release every attachment to the fall," is a general statement in case I was wrong about the reason I was stuck or in case I was stuck for more than one reason. This statement is also designed to quiet the remaining aches and pains since they are attached to the fall.

- Step 4 - Reinforce the truth. Like this, "I am here now, and I am safe. I love myself, and I am loved and protected by God."

- Step 5 - Ground yourself in the present moment by awakening your senses. Look in a mirror or notice the environment around you. Suck on ice or lemon. Hit a gong, play music, or just listen to the sounds around you. Smell a scent. Touch your hands together, feel your body. Let out the sound of your distraction. Awakening your senses can be used at any time to anchor yourself in the moment.

This process takes a few minutes, but the time it frees and the sense of presence and awareness that it facilitates make it worth the time.

Sensei Subira: What else should we know about using time?

Reverend Kelli: Habits, automatic behaviors, or what a coach friend of mine called, "running your racket," is another way of wasting time on the job and at home. It is reacting from past habit, rather than spiritually tuning in to the current circumstance and gleaning what authentic reaction, if any, is being called forth.

You want initiation of Divine connection to be so practiced that it becomes second nature and initiates itself automatically.

Sensei Subira: How do we interrupt ourselves when we are running our racket?

Reverend Kelli: If you are running your racket, you probably will not be able to interrupt yourself, because you will be acting unconsciously. If you become conscious of the fact that you are running your racket, your awareness itself will be an interrupter. The best way to interrupt your racket is to catch yourself when you are about to launch into it. It is the easy, lazy response, so look out for moments when you are feeling tired or overwhelmed, look out for moments when you are experiencing decision fatigue, these moments are ripe for running your racket, merely because you are too exhausted to remember and initiate Divine connection.

This is the reason to do your work! Because, just as when I fell, you want initiation of Divine connection to be so practiced that it becomes second nature and initiates itself automatically, even when (or especially when) you are tired or frazzled. In other words, you want to make connecting with God your racket, your natural go-to when life shows up and you are required to respond.

Sensei Subira: Make God my racket! Now, that is a good one.

Reverend Kelli: I promise you it is the best time hack of all!

It is Always a Good Time for God.
Release Resistance and Take the
Time to Lean Into The Divine.

Chapter

Free Yourself from the Groupthink Trap!

People dare not – they dare not turn the page. The laws of mimicry – I call them the laws of fear. People are afraid to find themselves alone, and don't find themselves at all.

~ André Gide ~

When all men think alike, no one thinks very much.

~ Walter Lippmann ~

Few are those who think with their own minds and feel with their own hearts.

~ Albert Einstein ~

Human progress is furthered, not by conformity, but by aberration.

~ H.L. Mencken ~

Lemmings do not commit mass suicide by following one another over cliffs. This is fake news created by a Disney movie where staging made it appear as if they were doing just that.[12] People, on the other hand, do commit a kind of mass suicide by following one another's thoughts and by killing their own will and creative impulses. This behavior is called groupthink! The day I had finished my first draft of this chapter, the Dictionary.com word of the day was groupthink. Because of this coincidence, blessing, or kismet, and because it offers a fitting introduction to the discussion in this chapter, I decided to add the definition here. Dictionary.com defines groupthink as, "the lack of individual creativity, or a sense of personal responsibility, that is sometimes characteristic of group interaction." With groupthink creativity and responsibility yield to group allegiance.

> *With groupthink creativity and responsibility yield to group allegiance.*

Groupthink becomes master, instead of Divinity.

> *The challenge is achieving conscious awareness, activating Spirit, and choosing courageously from that state of consciousness.*

To unleash Divinity at work you must overcome groupthink. In Matthew 6:24 Jesus offers this stern warning: "No one can serve two masters; for either he will hate the one and love the other, or he will be devoted to the one and despise the other. You cannot serve God and mammon." What is mammon? Mammon is money, possessions, fame, status, or whatever is valued more than God, including progress within the group or on the job. Doublemindedness obstructs Divine Expression. We cannot serve two masters. When the job says to do one thing and the deep beating heart of Spirit says do another, working can create a state of doublemindedness. You may long to succeed and desire to do the thing that will lead to your success but remember there is no true success without spiritual alignment!

Of course, most do not bow to an employer's every whim and do not completely abandon themselves to become who and what the job expects or desires. Instead, without being consciously aware of it or knowing why, when it counts, when the pressure is on, when God most needs a stand for truth, when the right thing is at risk, expression of Divine Self is impaired by the urge to conform. The good news is you can rise above the urge to conform if you understand it and apply Spirit to counter it.

Albert Einstein once said: "Great Spirits have always encountered violent opposition from mediocre minds. The mediocre mind is incapable of understanding the man who refuses to bow blindly to conventional prejudices and chooses instead to express his opinions courageously and honestly." I do not view conformity as an issue of mental mediocrity. The greatness of God exists within everyone and is available to be activated and called upon. Whether and to what degree we express Divinity is a choice. The challenge is not overcoming mental mediocrity. The challenge is achieving conscious awareness, activating Spirit, and choosing courageously from that state of consciousness.

This chapter takes a scientific look at the pressure to conform and outlines strategies for overcoming it. The next set of questions and answers addresses groupthink, an insurmountable challenge for many, but not for you who read this book! This chapter will tell you exactly how to overcome conformity![13]

Alright, it is time to break the spell of groupthink!

Sensei Subira: Reverend Kelli, I understand that groupthink is another great challenge that people should be looking out for if they are attempting to be more spiritual at work. Will you tell us about this challenge?

Reverend Kelli: Absolutely! Sensei, have you ever been told: "Well, this is our policy," or "Well, that's just the rule," as a reason that is supposed to justify some unfairness or injustice that is occurring?

Groupthink is not thinking at all. It is a stand-in for thinking. Groupthink is the regurgitation of decisions previously made by the employer.

Sensei Subira: Yes, it is common. It is frustrating. We have all had that experience. How does that connect?

Reverend Kelli: Those responses are a product of groupthink!

Sensei Subira: Groupthink is a familiar term. I have heard it mentioned in a lot of different contexts. Tell us exactly what you mean, Reverend Kelli.

Reverend Kelli: When I say groupthink, I am describing a state that is disengaged from Spirit. Thinking is a Divine Process. Groupthink is not thinking at all. It is a stand-in for thinking. Groupthink is the regurgitation of decisions previously made by the employer.

As an example, let us examine Jesus' interaction with the religious leaders of his time.

Sensei Subira: Is this a Christian doctrine? And for that matter, Reverend Kelli, are you a Christian? I know that you often quote Biblical Scripture.

Reverend Kelli: Okay, this is a great place to address that. I love Jesus, and I focus on the aspects of Jesus and the Bible that I love. I accept that which enhances, enriches, and deepens my relationship with God. I prefer not to argue about my beliefs, or whether the Bible or Christianity is flawed. I am inspired by Jesus and his journey, I am inspired by aspects of Christianity and many other religions, and from each, I use what supports my relationship with God (emphasis on the word *my*). I am a zealous believer in the personal nature of my relationship with God. I do not let religious groupthink control that relationship.

Sensei Subira: Religious groupthink, I love it! I hear you Reverend Kelli, but you know there are folks out there who are going to want a direct answer. Are you a Christian?

Reverend Kelli: Well, I will ask, was Jesus a Christian? How do we define a Christian? And, who gets to define it? My deep love of Jesus and the teachings of Jesus make me both Christian and not Christian, because at the deepest, most fundamental levels of my practice, the teachings of Jesus take me far outside modern-day Christianity, into freedom and unconditional love.

If Christian means the Bible and Jesus are my primary sources of spiritual inspiration outside of Spirit itself, then I am Christian. If Christian means that I was baptized in one of the multiple Christian denominations, then I am Christian. I have gone through the process that some call being "saved," because that was the ritual at the church I attended.

Sensei Subira: You were raised in church?

Reverend Kelli: I was raised in Allen Chapel, African Methodist Episcopal Church. That is the church of my birth family. I attended Catholic school for a bit, and Catholicism is significant to me; some in my family are Catholic. I married the stepson of a Pentecostal minister and explored that denomination a bit. I have been drawn to Buddhism since I was exposed to it at a young age through close family friends. And, during the past decade or so, I have explored Hinduism. Still, Jesus is my role model and my love, not for the miracles, but his daring; for his love of the unloved, for his wisdom, and for the generous offering that he made of himself.

> *More than founding a religion, Jesus demonstrated a way of engaging religion.*

He gave himself away! He gave us new knowledge and understanding of God as beautiful and loving. To all of this, I aspire. More than founding a religion, Jesus demonstrated a way of engaging religion.

Jesus was Jewish. He followed the sacred traditions of Judaism. He was a teacher with disciples. He taught his disciples, but whether what he taught was Judaism is where things get a little murky. His interactions with Jewish leaders demonstrated that His understanding of and relationship with God extended beyond the naked tenets and practices of any religion, beyond Judaism, and beyond what we now call Christianity. He lived, taught, and interpreted the law, not just from a place of connection and inspiration, but from a place of oneness. He understood that God is too big to fit within the confines of religion. And He admitted that not all aspects of God's plan were known to Him (Mathew 24:36). One of my challenges with religion and religious teachers is the attempt to explain everything. Why not thrive in the mystery? I cannot explain everything, and I am not interested in trying to do so.

Sensei Subira: So, I think I am sensing the connection, but I will ask you to spell it out. How does Jesus relate to groupthink?

Reverend Kelli: Jesus lived His whole life in defiance of groupthink! I mean, look at Him: as a kid straying away from His mother and father and then claiming to be about His Father's business (Luke 2:49); later defending and hanging out with women of poor reputation (Luke 7:36-50) (John 7:53-8:11); then healing on the Sabbath day (Mark 3:1-6), and forgiving sins (Matthew 9:1-8) (Mark 2:1-12). Let us remember, Jesus was executed for blasphemy and treason because His approach to religious practice so offended the religious leaders of the day and so threatened Roman officials (Mark 61-64) (Luke 23:2).

Sensei Subira: No doubt, Jesus thought for Himself!

Reverend Kelli: He did! He stood in His Divine Identity so strongly that people found it threatening and blasphemous. He took on the danger of this and paid the consequences. And He told us we would do things greater than He did, but we must daily take up our cross (John 14:12) (Luke 9:23; Matthew 10:38).

Connected thinking is a form of Divine expression.

Part of taking up the cross is being willing to stand in Divine Identity. You are to connect and let Spirit filter itself through the unique apparatus of your mind, an apparatus tempered by the unique continuum of your experiences. When you connect with Spirit and think a thought, that thought is the product of your Divinity and is uniquely your own.

Connected thinking is a form of Divine expression.

You are here to generate this form of expression, and through it, you are to add value and beauty to the collective mosaic of Divinity.

Divinity enters the room because someone reveals it.

When you give yourself over to groupthink, what you would authentically offer to the job through your Divine faculty remains missing. Instead of listening through your open portal to Spirit and offering what you hear, you listen without. Groupthink hijacks the process, and through it, the job receives and operates out of the redundant regurgitation of one thought.

Sensei Subira: Is that always a bad thing?

Reverend Kelli: Instead of labeling it bad, think about it as incomplete. With groupthink, rather than a marketplace of ideas that can be mixed and matched, there is no multiplicity or diversity; there is only repetition and duplication of thoughts that themselves may not have resulted from connected thinking. Divinity enters the room because someone reveals it.

A project can be completed in a billion different ways. The way it is completed will depend on the vibration of the people completing it. The assignment is to stand in the room, vibrate from the highest level of consciousness available, and then influence the outcome. If we are too afraid or too hypnotized by conformity to offer what God has placed us in the room to offer, then our contribution is missing. There is always something missing when we fail to think our own thoughts and exercise our own will. In one sense, when we fail to think and exercise our Divine faculty of will, we become less Divine and less human. We become less alive and more inanimate.

Sensei Subira: If not thinking, what are people doing on the job? How are they getting caught up in groupthink? What happens to them to make them vulnerable to it?

Reverend Kelli: Great questions! The answer is that most jobs subtly or openly promote groupthink. Vision statements, mission statements, mottos, policies, rules, codes of conduct, rewards, punishments, and hierarchies entrain employees and influence their behavior. When I was training to be a speaker, I learned that having a group engage in three activities where everyone is asked to do the same thing creates a synchronized energy field that makes the impact of the talk more powerful. Social Influence Theories offer tools for influencing the thoughts and actions of target audiences. These strategies are employed by companies to influence their customers and employees.

It is easy to fall into the trap of behaving in ways that other people have predesigned. For example, I do not work for the cable company, but because the telephone technician tells me it will help her fix my cable problem, I let her direct me to get on the floor, read serial numbers, perform self-tests, and tighten loose cables. The grocery store offers the reward of getting out of the store faster if I engage in the behavior of checking and bagging my own groceries, and I do it, with little thought about the fact that it is their responsibility to hire enough employees so I get out of the store quickly. As a paying customer, I deserve efficient check-out and bagging, but I do not get it, and I do not insist on it. How do they get away with this? Ask the guys who once made a living pumping gas! The more work a company can outsource to its customers, the fewer employees it has to hire. And good people sit on implementation teams, in board rooms, and executive planning meetings causing and allowing all this to go on.

> *A company man is someone who commits and fits.*

Sensei Subira: I remember hearing the term *company man*. Is this what we are talking about?

Reverend Kelli: That is right! A company man is someone who commits and fits.

It is evident from how he dresses, speaks, and allots his time, everything about him reeks of the company. Today we could add the term *company woman* to the lexicon. I remember being very conscious of how I fit in. Was I dressed properly, carrying myself properly, and, as a Black Woman, code-switching properly?[14]

In the law firm, there was an unspoken and sometimes spoken expectation. The same is true in corporations and other jobs. Employees unconsciously (and sometimes consciously) adapt to expectations and adopt a hive mind. Like the Borg in the Star Trek series, they become less like people and more like cyborgs or automatons. They behave as one, as the company, and according to the company's pre-established dictates. This is true even in creative industries like media and entertainment; there is a pattern in the stories told and the vantage point from which they are told. That pattern is the result of groupthink.

Few, if any, jobs are free from pressure to conform. If you choose to overcome conformity, it is up to you to ground yourself in energy more powerful than the external pressure. Spirit is that energy!

Groupthink is an indoctrination that begins when we are toddlers. Parents and others teach us to know and follow *the rules* and that there is a "price to pay" for not obeying. The job, a microcosm of the greater society, is just dutifully continuing the droning process. When it comes to punishment, execution and ostracism are society's big guns. The job's equivalents are firing and blackballing. It follows, then, that fear of punishment and other psychological states keep employees in line despite over 100 Scriptural directives to fear not and be not afraid.

Sensei Subira: Well, we all know about fear and how it impacts us on the job. Tell us about the other psychological states.

Reverend Kelli: The states I am referring to are conformity and the agentic state. Let us look at conformity first. Let me say, I am no psychologist. I wear many hats, but not that one! This will not be a deep dive. If people want to go deeper, I invite them to do more research. There is a lot of publicly available information out there on conformity and the agentic state.

Sensei Subira: That is what I do! When a topic is important to me, I do my research so I can assess its value and accuracy myself.

With that understood, Reverend Kelli, tell us what you have learned about conformity.

Reverend Kelli: Sensei, I am going to talk about a couple of experiments that show how conformity works. You may have heard of the 1971 Stanford Prison Experiment. It was funded by the military and studied how people behave when they are given power.

Sensei Subira: I think I may have heard of it.

Reverend Kelli: It is known for the fact that randomly chosen, and presumably moral, college students were transformed into brutes when an authority assigned them roles to play.

Sensei Subira: Stanford did this study or the military?

Reverend Kelli: The Navy paid for it. A psychologist named Philip Zimbardo; a Stanford professor led it. A movie called *The Stanford Prison Experiment* was made about it. Zimbardo later wrote a book on the experiment. The book includes three decades of subsequent research about what causes good people to behave immorally. It is called *The Lucifer Effect*, and it also examines the 2003 prisoner abuse in Abu Ghraib.

Sensei Subira: We have all heard of how the Abu Ghraib prisoners were treated. What happened in the Stanford Experiment?

Reverend Kelli: Certain student participants were given power and lost themselves in abuse. Other students suffered at the mercy of these power abusers and reacted.

Here is how it worked. Students were assigned to be guards or prisoners. The lab was a mini prison built for the experiment. The idea was to study the behavior between guards and prisoners, where all participants were aware their roles were not real. The guards knew they were not real guards and the prisoners knew they were not real prisoners.

> *People conform even when no one tells them specifically what to do.*

Sensei Subira: And?

Reverend Kelli: The students directed to play the role of guard brutally abused the students directed to play the role of prisoner, to such a degree that the study had to be stopped. The conclusion was that people do not think. People conform. People conform even when no one tells them specifically what to do.

They conform to the roles given to them by authority figures, even if their interpretation of those roles requires them to engage in morally questionable behavior.

Sensei Subira: Wow that is crazy! So, when someone takes on the role of boss, or manager, or supervisor, or whatever their role, they naturally tend toward becoming the worse version of that?

Reverend Kelli: That question gets to the heart of it. Power can be used benevolently or malevolently.

Sensei Subira: What is it that makes the difference in what one chooses?

Reverend Kelli: Spirit! And even though it is that simple, it is also more complicated. Let us talk a little about a second experiment, which occurred earlier, back in the 1950s.

Sensei Subira: That is way back!

Reverend Kelli: Yes! All the experiments we will be discussing happened years ago. They are seminal experiments, meaning they laid the foundation for much of the predominant thinking on conformity and the agentic state.

Sensei Subira: What are the other experiments?

Reverend Kelli: The next one is called the Asch Paradigm. It was conducted by Psychologist Solomon Asch and measured the impact of peer pressure on conformity. Eight people were placed in seats around a table. Seven were working with the experimenters and only pretending to be subjects, let us refer to them as *fake subjects*. The eighth, the only one not working with the experimenters, was the true subject.

Sensei Subira: They used seven fake subjects to test the reactions of one true subject? Tricky!

Reverend Kelli: Yes, social scientists do a lot of false set-ups to isolate and test reactions. Also, this was not just one group of eight people. They experimented on multiple groups of eight to ensure accurate results. All total there were eighty-seven true subjects, fifty of whom were exposed to peer pressure and thirty-seven in the control group, who were not exposed to peer pressure.

> *Consistent with Social Identity Theory, individuals obey authorities they identify with and believe to be right.*

In the experiment, the fake subjects gave pre-set answers to questions. The goal was to see how the behavior of the fake subjects would influence the answers given by the test subject who was free to choose a different answer. The experimenters varied the amount of peer pressure by varying the tone and certainty with which the fake subjects offered the preset answers. The questions were objective and had nothing to do with moral issues. The correct answers were obvious and related to the length of lines on a card.

When the fake subjects were asked questions about which line was longest, or which line matched the length of another line, they first gave correct answers, but gradually, they added a sprinkling of incorrect answers. This let experimenters see how the answers of the true subject would change when his peers' answers changed.

Sensei Subira: Do not tell me people gave wrong answers just because other people did?

Reverend Kelli: They did!

> *Also, if even one other person disagreed with the wrong answer given by the majority, subjects were 80% less likely to succumb to peer pressure.*

When experimenters tested subjects not exposed to peer pressure, less than 1% gave the wrong answer. When exposed to peer pressure 74% of the subjects gave a wrong answer to at least one question. Only 26% of subjects never conformed to wrong answers

It is not surprising that peer pressure can cause conformity, but these results astounded me!

Here is a powerful nugget for the work that we are doing in this book. Follow-ups to the Asch work concluded that the number of people giving wrong answers and the forcefulness with which the wrong answers were given made a difference to the results. One incorrect voice made little difference to the answers, but the influence steadily increased if two or three people repeated the wrong answer. Also, if even one other person disagreed with the wrong answer given by the majority, subjects were 80% less likely to succumb to peer pressure.

The experiment showed that it is much more difficult to resist the majority if you are alone in your opinion, but one additional voice can make all the difference. Anonymity also made a difference. Subjects were able to resist the pressure to answer incorrectly if they were allowed to give their answers anonymously.

Sensei Subira: This is fascinating!

Reverend Kelli: It is! Now let me tell you about the agentic state. The agentic state is similar to conformity but adds a slight twist. The idea is that instead of being accountable for bad behavior, the actor can pivot away from accountability and shift moral blame to an authority.

Sensei Subira: How does that work, Reverend Kelli?

Reverend Kelli: Corporations and other jobs inadvertently or willfully entrain employees to obey their rules and ways of being. Employees become automated and the job's rules and policies become their operating system as if the employer had programmed them. This automated mindset disempowers the employees and renders them virtually incapable of using their own will, creativity, judgment, and discretion. In the agentic state, individuality, accountability, and willpower are nonexistent. The employee essentially is an automaton, willing to obey whatever orders are given by the employer.

> *Evil is easy to swallow in small bites. When evil happens incrementally, it is almost invisible, particularly to those who have no interest in seeing it.*

Even if Spirit is telling the employee to do what is in the highest good, the employee may turn a deaf ear because he is entrained to follow a rule that is telling him to do something different. The employee may not even be able to develop a creative solution to address a problem right in front of him, because his creativity is impaired by the existence and operation of the rule.

The agentic state is defined as an emotional or mental condition that occurs when people who work beneath the authority of others, within a bureaucracy based on status, are motivated to follow commands issued by their superiors. [15]

So, the agentic state, groupthink, and automatism are the things we need to look out for when we are on the job. We need to make sure that instead of becoming a robot, we stay a Divine Being.

Sensei Subira: "Superiors!" Now there is a word for you!

Reverend Kelli: It is! Words matter. When the job calls a supervisor an employee's superior, no one can feign surprise when that employee ends up believing he is to be obedient and follow that supervisor's commands. Feeling "less than" positions an employee to abandon his or her Divine Identity and the faculties that accompany it.

The agentic state adds the idea that the employee is an agent of the employer. Agency theory is a legal theory that shields employees from legal culpability for certain actions taken on behalf of the employer. Psychologist Stanley Milgram found that the concept of agency has psychological consequences.

Milgram's experiment, conducted in the sixties, is the most famous of the conformity experiments. In light of World War II atrocities, Milgram wanted to determine whether the Nazis involved were strangely obedient or whether ordinary people under the right set of conditions would do the same thing.

Sensei Subira: I am afraid to hear what happened.

Reverend Kelli: The results were shocking! Sorry, Sensei, in a minute, you will see what a bad pun that was. Milgram's experiment asked subjects to administer shocks.

Milgram advertised to the public that he was conducting a memory study. He assigned volunteers the role of "Teacher," and asked the Teachers to shock "Learners" whom the teachers believed to be volunteers also. A Teacher was to shock a Learner whenever the Learner failed to remember the correct answer. The Teachers were told that with every wrong answer, shocks would increase in magnitude from 15 V to 450 V in 15 V increments.

Sensei Subira: Wait a minute, 450 V? That sounds like a deadly level of electricity!

Reverend Kelli: Good observation, Sensei! Depending on a person's health, a 450 V shock could be deadly or at least cause excruciating pain and difficulty breathing. In this case, there were no real shocks. As I said, the Learners were in on the experiment and were only pretending to feel pain. And they were great pretenders! The Learners screamed and begged for the "shocks" to stop. Teachers could hear the Learners, but in most cases, with light prompting from the experimenter, they continued to push the button they believed to be causing the Learners to experience shocks. The

Milgram experiment's true purpose was to test how far the Teachers would go. In the original version of the experiment, all Teachers went so far as to deliver shocks of 300 V and 65% of the Teachers went all the way to 450 V.

From the Milgram experiment, a common belief developed that the majority of the population is willing to kill simply because an authority orders them to do so.

Sensei Subira: That is incredible! I cannot imagine myself or anyone I know doing that!

Reverend Kelli: That is what most of us would say, but the experiment shows that most of us would administer the shocks under similar conditions. This really tells the story: when Milgram debriefed Teachers, he praised them for their commitment to the advancement of science, especially when it had caused them to feel uncomfortable. The debriefing erased participants' doubts. The typical response after the debriefing was that stated by one Teacher: "I am happy to have been of service," and, "Continue your experiments by all means as long as good can come of them. In this crazy mixed-up world of ours, every bit of goodness is needed." Tragically, this little bit of post-experiment reinforcement led Teachers to dismiss obvious moral concerns arising from their behavior and to convince themselves that they were doing good.

It is easy to see how this kind of cycle could exist on a job and lead employees to do things in the heat of the moment, or the heat of their career, that in retrospect they feel ashamed or guilty about.

Sensei Subira: It seems like some are willing to believe whatever makes them feel better about themselves.

Reverend Kelli: Especially if an authority figure generates the feel-good fiction.

Sensei Subira: Is this another way that mindless obedience impacts us?

Reverend Kelli: Great question. Maybe. As we have talked about, generally it is accepted that the behavior of the subjects in these experiments demonstrates a mindless surrender to the will of governing structures. But another theory contends that the behavior reflects the opposite. According to this other theory, the Milgram experiment is not about blind conformity; it is about people doing something they believe is important, helping to advance science.

Sensei Subira: Wow, that view is miles apart from the agentic state theory.

Reverend Kelli: It is! The alternative view is that people internalize roles and rules as aspects of a system with which they identify.

So, if a person identifies with the system of scientific experimentation, that person will be willing to adopt the roles and rules of scientific experimentation and use those roles and rules as a guide in determining their own actions. Thus, the theory holds "the hallmark of tyrannical regimes is not conformity but creative leadership and engaged followership within a group of true believers."

Sensei Subira: Do the experiments support this alternative view?

Reverend Kelli: Supporters of the theory claim that they do. Supporters point out that variants in the Milgram experiment that diminished the degree to which subjects identified with experimenters also diminished the degree of conformity. For example, when Milgram moved the experiment to commercial premises that were not as swanky or prestigious as the Yale University labs, conformity decreased. These theorists suggest that consistent with Social Identity Theory, individuals obey authorities they identify with and believe to be right.

Sensei Subira: How do the World War II atrocities line up with the alternative view?

Reverend Kelli: Again, it depends on what you believe motivated the behavior of the Nazis. Advocates of the alternative theory believe Nazi bureaucrats were aware of what they were doing and believed it to be right. They point to a statement

Rules and roles sometimes cause good people to act in bad or idiotic ways.

by a bureaucrat that his "one regret was that he had not killed more Jews." This attitude of "commitment to the cause" is similar to the Teachers in Milgram's experiments, who easily shifted away from upset over their actions to a view that their actions were a "service" in the cause of "goodness."

Sensei Subira: Reverend Kelli, how do we reconcile the differences in these two theories?

Reverend Kelli: We cannot, Sensei! The good thing is, we do not have to! We only need to know a few bottom-line points. The first is that rules and roles sometimes cause good people to act in bad or idiotic ways.

Jobs routinely tell employees to accept the authority of anonymous unseen others who have decided how the company, and its employees, ought to behave under various circumstances. The typical employee does not set these rules but is expected to abide by them, to encourage others to abide by them and to impose them on others.

Second, employees who have no idea where the rules come from or why a given rule is the rule, still frequently feel invested personally in enforcing the rules. Maybe these employees are mindlessly surrendering to an authority above them because they feel like they have no personal power or discretion to override rules. Maybe, like automatons, their brains are operating automatically, as if the rules are an algorithm controlling their behavior. On the other hand, maybe they are zealously enforcing the policies of an authority they identify with and believe to be right.

Sensei Subira: Why does it not matter?

Reverend Kelli: It does not matter because the process for overriding or avoiding programming is the same.

This chapter is called groupthink. Regardless of how an employee arrives at groupthink, whether he is there from powerlessness and surrender or choice and identification, whether she is there because she has been entrained by her employer or because she is driven to climb the corporate ladder, it does not matter. I want everyone reading this book to be empowered to avoid groupthink altogether.

Sensei Subira: That seems easier said than done.

Reverend Kelli: No, it is as easily done as said. This chapter has been longer and more complex than most, not because the solution is complicated, but because the problem is. It is a serious problem with potentially devastating effects, as the Nazis have shown us, and as all the so-called "crimes of obedience" have shown us. When accountability for wrongdoing can be broadly dispersed, when it can be assigned to a nonexistent entity (the corporation) that all the actors can hide behind, when it can be dressed up and made to seem good instead of bad, no matter the moral quandary, it becomes easy to play a small role without guilt or regret. Evil is easy to swallow in small bites. When evil happens incrementally, it is almost invisible, particularly to those who have no interest in seeing it.

This chapter is about being on the lookout, watching yourself and your influences, making sure the good you do, which you think is good, actually is good.

Sensei Subira: So, this chapter is a warning?

Reverend Kelli: It is! Sensei. In the days of firing squads, it is said that the government would ensure that one member of the squad was shooting a blank round. This was done to provide a sort of plausible deniability for the entire squad. This was not because they needed to deny their actions to others. Their actions were protected by law. It was so that they could deny their actions when they had to confront themselves. After all, they had shot and killed another human being who was restrained and who had caused them no harm. The plausible deniability was to soothe their consciences. As you previously pointed out, we will tell ourselves whatever we need to tell ourselves to feel okay with what we have done or are doing. The blank round gave everyone on the squad the opportunity to doubt that they had participated in the kill. The blank round had empowered each of them to look through the sight at the target over the heart of their victim and fire.

> *You never have to worry about surrendering to a job or acquiring a corporate identity if you have already surrendered to God and grounded yourself in your Divine Identity.*

Sensei Subira: Wow! What an odyssey! We have come full circle.

Reverend Kelli: Not quite yet. Full circle brings us back to the practice, back to our anchor, back to Divine Identity. You see, you never have to worry about surrendering to a job or acquiring a corporate identity if you have already surrendered to God and grounded yourself in your Divine Identity.

This is the path! This is the wow, the destination of the odyssey, and the completion of the circle.

Sensei Subira: All the experiments boil down to this?

Reverend Kelli: They do. We fulfill our calling by standing in Divine Identity. It is how we are to participate in God's Divine Experiment. And, as the conformity experiments have shown, when we stand in Divine Identity and express our authentic voice, our voice empowers everyone in the room to break free. It shatters illusions and breaks entrainment. It overrides the programming and reminds others that they too have Divine Faculties, they too have a Divine Identity, and they too have the power to choose authentically.

> *Divine Identity Shields. Stand in It*
> *and Empower Yourself and Others*
> *to Rise Above All False Influences.*

Chapter

Walk the Sacred Path of the Spirituality-at-Work Champion

The whole point of education is to teach by example.

~ Jacques Turgot ~

From now on I will make burning my aim, for I am like a candle: burning only makes me brighter.

~ Jalaluddin Rumi ~

There is little sense in attempting to change external conditions; you must first change inner beliefs, then outer conditions will change accordingly.

~ Brian Adams ~

Real people have made real progress through the activity of Spirit at work. I say *the activity of Spirit* because processes and tools are useless without the activity of Spirit. The kind of transformation discussed in this book involves Spirit.

Spirit is operating always, whether we are doing anything to stir it or not. It is always leaning toward us even as we are yearning to experience it. The yearning is evidence of the leaning. You are here reading this, because now, right where you are, Spirit is leaning toward you, attracting you to your destiny, your True Work, and your Divine Self.

Spirit is identity. But for the most part, life has coerced and indoctrinated us to abandon identity in favor of acceptability. Abandoning our identity as Spirit causes us to create a mimicked reality, meaning we lend our creative power to realities others are creating and believing should or do exist. Then, these realities feel like a trap we cannot escape. Spiritual connection reveals with stunning clarity the places in our lives where we are living in a way that is misaligned. So, if you connect, you will see, then you will choose what it is your destiny to create. This is how Spirit frees you to become your destiny. Essentially, Spirit is the butterfly inside you, always quietly prodding and positioning you to release your caterpillar ways. In this respect, you can think of the job as a cocoon. It can be a place where the caterpillar dissolves and the magic and mysticism of Spirit make you the butterfly you are meant to become.

Beware, caterpillars sometimes die painful deaths. Spiritual emergence can be bloody and uncomfortable and feel more like hell than heaven. It can be rough for a long time before it is smooth and easy. Stay in it for the long haul and you will experience unimaginable beauty. Then, when you look to see what is so breathtaking, you will be surprised to discover it is you; it is what Spirit is even now becoming as you.

In this section, we will look at real people and their real on-the-job experiences. Each one has involved spiritual emergence. And, that emergence has occurred in the setting of the job. Their experiences illustrate what it looks like, all the moving parts, and what it can become when all the dust settles. I see them as champions. You may see them in the same way or even view their experiences as a template for your emergence. I am proud to include myself among them.

In any case, I am confident that, like me, you will find their stories inspiring!

Sensei Subira: Reverend Kelli, maybe there is a story you can tell or an example that sums up what good things can come from experiencing God on the job, experiencing your Divinity at work?

Reverend Kelli: Yes, I have already shared a bit of my own story and I will share a little more. Then, I will share the stories of others who, for me, are spirituality-at-work champions. Each of these people has had their work lives drastically changed by the activity of Spirit. I know these people personally. Their stories are true. And, through their stories, you will learn how Spirit actively worked within their lives and completely changed their work environments.

First things first: here is my story.

REVEREND KELLI'S STORY

> *Throughout my career, Spirit has provided similar choice points, moments where making the spiritually aligned choice paid material dividends.*

It began with signs, symbols, and synchronicities. The on-campus interview for my first job was rudely interrupted by the extremely late arrival of the person scheduled to interview ahead of me. She showed up harried, sweating, full of excuses and apologies, and yet, demanding to be interviewed. Unfortunately, the interviewer had no time to interview us both. He had an appointment back at the office and two more interviews to do after lunch. But, this woman was persistent; she would not take no for an answer and we appeared to have a stalemate. I solved the problem creatively. I ceded the rest of the interview time to her and asked if I could have lunch with the interviewer. He agreed, and the result was a callback and a job offer. Arguably, the creative problem solving and cooperativeness I demonstrated won over the interviewer; yet, I am clear that Spirit presented me with a ripe circumstance to show myself, to do right, and to make a strong positive impression. Throughout my career, Spirit has provided similar choice points, moments where making the spiritually aligned choice paid material dividends.

I learned of my cravings for money and status. I learned of my ability to forgive and my tolerance for humiliating circumstances. I processed my fears, my cutoff point, and the depths of my faith. And I grew! I grew in my love for God and my trust in God. I grew in my connection to God and my yearning to connect. Every step of the way, God met me, led me, amazed me, and did incredible work through me.

It was a process. Many of my cravings were healed through disappointment that felt like suffering. But, in the end, I received what I valued most and what is now mine to give: freedom. I have the freedom to see myself as I am, to be myself as I am and as I am becoming, and the freedom to fearlessly allow Spirit to have its perfect way (most of the time). For me, *this is the most satisfying, gratifying success, and it is a success grounded in the hope of more, deeper, fuller, and better to come.*

Sensei Subira: If you could sum it up with a single sentence, what would that sentence be?

Reverend Kelli: Hmm, okay. Here it is: Through beauty, pain, poverty, prosperity, God grows us toward becoming us with every experience on and off the job!

Sensei Subira: Perfect! I love it! Who is next?

Reverend Kelli: The next story is about a former coaching client. She was a dentist and was very unhappy about the people at the job where she was working. She believed that contrary to her internal ethical code, she was being asked to put money above people. When she began to open and experience her Divine Self, her True Work, everything changed. Mind you, it is not like the whole workplace magically changed because she changed, but God did usher her into the place where she belongs, where she can stand and say, "I am going to be the truth of who I am." Here is her story.

DR. J'S STORY

I remember when I first fell in love with the idea of becoming a dentist. I was a sophomore in college, and I attended an "Impressions" program held at the dental school. I was impressed to find a profession that combined my interest in health and art. I was more impressed to see female dental students, who looked like me, becoming dentists. I was encouraged, motivated, and inspired by these women. When I got back to my dorm room, I remember feeling overjoyed and excited about my realization that dentistry was my chosen profession, and with that, I embarked on the journey of becoming a dentist.

Once I accomplished my goal, holding my degree as a Doctor of Dental Surgery, I imagined that I had made it. I imagined that my life would now look and feel like the success I spent many challenging years working to attain. To my surprise, it did not.

Yes, I was grateful for the many fruits of my accomplishments. I was under 30 with a 6-figure salary, and I was enjoying having the means to afford things I was not able to before. My parents put an ad in our local newspaper congratulating me on my accomplishments. It felt good, making my parents proud and making my family, my community, and myself proud. On the surface, everything looked like success; everything was perfect, and I was good at being who I thought I should be, what others expected of me.

I did excellent dental work for my patients, according to what I had been taught in school. It was clear I was very well-liked by my patients, staff, and colleagues. I quickly ascended to a lead dentist position, running a solo practice in the company I worked for. But that did not last long. Six months later, I left the company and it would be another 8 months before I would practice dentistry again. What went wrong? The surface was a lie, and while so-called success was apparent on the outside, on the inside, I was falling apart. I questioned if I had made the right choice in becoming a dentist.

Why was this level of success not bringing me joy?

The truth was, I did not know myself, my true self, and as a result, I did not know what I wanted in life. I operated like a well-programmed robot. I would go from room to room, spend a few minutes talking with my patients, and following a script of what to diagnose and treat based on what I learned in school. Working in the environment of our conventional health care system did not work for me because I was not created to check boxes and fulfill quotas while pleasing everyone in the process. I discovered I was created to facilitate deeper healing—the healing our society is in desperate need of.

Fortunately, I chose to invest in myself by getting a spiritual life coach, Reverend Kelli. I began the journey towards self-discovery; and as I spent years doing inner healing work, I realized the true purpose behind my gift of being a dentist. My healing journey forced me to discover for myself what it means to be a health practitioner: I was born to be a healer and a teacher by being a doctor. Being a dentist is a gift from God. I am a chosen one; God works through me to bring healing to others in a way only I can. I learned holistic approaches to healing. I learned that healing means to make whole, and that requires work on all levels of existence. I began to question what I was taught to believe was the best way to practice dentistry and why it was the standard of care. I could not just treat a tooth and be satisfied with the results. I was being called to be a healing presence for each person I encountered at work: my patients, my staff, my colleagues. Once connected with Source and making conscious choices to live in alignment with my truth, I created a dream workplace that reflected my inner healing work.

I did not have to build it from scratch; in fact, it was waiting for me. After three nudges from different people in my spiritual community, it was clear I was being guided to meet with a particular dentist. This dentist owned the practice that would eventually become my work home. And, it definitely feels like home.

At my current practice, we are a family. I have meaningful connections with the staff, my patients, and my colleagues. We begin every workday with a centering practice to set the tone for our day in service to our patients. Now I take pride in being fully present for my patients during their time with me. I listen to their needs and create a safe space for their healing. In addition to the dental work, I sit and talk to my patients about the importance of their diet and the impact it has on their health. I explain what I see in their mouth, what it could mean on all levels of their existence. I encourage them to ask questions and to check within for their answers. In the chair, we talk, laugh, sing, cry, and talk about what is going on in their life that might affect why their tooth is hurting. I take my time, as opposed to just declaring that the tooth needs a root canal.

I spend most of my time at work laughing and singing, the staff will tell you. I have never worked anywhere where I felt this comfortable being all of who I am. At work, I am a dentist . . . and I am also a coach, a teacher, a friend, and even a rapper when I show that side of me. I am evolving as a leader in this practice and playing a significant role in evolving the practice to greater heights. I love where I work now because I love who I am and who I am becoming. I love what I do now because I find purpose in how I do what I do, and it is only the beginning.

Sensei Subira: That is an amazing story! I am inspired!

Reverend Kelli: I am telling you, seeing how God shows up in our lives is a bible in itself. Sensei, I think you are going to recognize this next story. It is about a good friend and a fellow minister. After issues of worthiness and trust had polluted her work experience, I watched her and supported her in being accountable for the changes she desired to experience. She consistently applied tools and processed herself and her experiences to create her current work experience. Now, her job looks exactly like what she envisioned. She is valued, she is free, and she is doing meaningful work.

And now, in her own words, Reverend A!

REVEREND A'S STORY

I am clear that my spiritual practices have kept me employed and allowed me to flourish on the job. Years ago, I would not have believed it possible for me to experience my current level of job success and fulfillment. In fact, at one point, I was doubtful that I would make it to the next year with my employer.

Negative experiences with a co-worker-turned-boss led to anger, a lack of trust, feeling on the outside, and fearing I was on my way out. As two of my co-workers with similar experiences made their way out the door for the last time, I knew I needed to make a change if I did not want to take the same walk myself. I was clear I wanted to leave the company on my terms when I was ready, and at the time of these events, I was not ready yet.

> *Consistent with the Radical Forgiveness principles, I remained open to the idea that "the boss" and I had co-created what we were experiencing to heal a wound that existed in each of us.*

I did what I thought was spiritually responsible and started a conversation about trust. "I know that we have a problem with trust between us, and I plan to do my part to change that," I began. While my mouth was still open to continue speaking, "the boss" said, "I don't have a problem trusting you." "Okay," I said to myself, "this is going to be harder than I thought. 'The boss' is either unable to see it or unwilling to own it."

As I had recently completed my ministerial and metaphysical studies, I decided to own my part and take the lead in shifting my energy. I believed that shifting my energy would shift the energy around me. I prayed, I meditated, and I tried some new practices.

I had learned about Radical Forgiveness in my ministerial studies and felt that my situation at work could benefit from a good dose of forgiveness. Consistent with the Radical Forgiveness principles, I remained open to the idea that "the boss" and I had co-created what we were experiencing to heal a wound that existed in each of us.

This perspective helped me see "the boss" as my healing angel rather than my enemy. I used the process to clear my anger and fear around the situation and to shift my vision of "the boss" enough to show up differently at work.

> I was able to release the fear of being asked to leave. I knew that I had succeeded in creating an atmosphere where I felt in charge of deciding to stay or go on my timetable.

I also drew a manifestation wheel, a technique I learned in a book about the teachings of Abraham (as shared by Ester and Jerry Hicks). As described in the book, I drew two circles in a clock-like arrangement. In the smaller, center circle, I stated my intention to elevate my energy and the energy around me on the job to the level that supported my continuation in that position. Around the larger second circle, where clock numbers might have been, I wrote statements that I knew to be true, statements that supported my intention. I put my manifestation wheel in a place where I could see and read it from time to time. I also deepened my commitment to my regular spiritual practices.

The energy on the job continuously shifted until eventually, it reached the point where I was able to release the fear of being asked to leave.

I knew that I had succeeded in creating an atmosphere where I felt in charge of deciding to stay or go on my timetable.

A year or so later, "the boss" decided to move on to another type of work.

As I write this about 8 years later, I celebrate the choices I made and the actions I took to change my experience and to continue my employment with the company. I am so grateful!

Today, the atmosphere on the job is completely different, as is my role in our work. My position with the company has grown to senior management level with much of the staff reporting to departments I direct. This moment is the juiciest time of my tenure. I stayed to participate in a shift in focus that I wanted to see from the beginning, and I feel blessed to take part in the contributions we are making in our community. In the past, "the boss" *had accused me of trying to run my ministry out of our company, and as a result, I felt hesitant to show that side of myself. Today, I sit at the same desk I sat at years ago, but my relationship with the job is completely different. I have created a new work experience that welcomes all of me, and to that experience, I bring my full self, especially my spiritual self. From this mutual exchange I benefit and my job benefits. My day job supports my spiritual work, and my spiritual work returns the blessing.*

Sensei Subira: Wow! I did not know Reverend A's story!

Reverend Kelli: It is powerful! And I know of at least a half dozen other stories that I could have included here that would have been equally powerful. That is how amazing God is and how consistently God shows up on our job and in our career when we invite God in. Sometimes, God shows up even when we do not.

The next work champion is a man I have not known as long but feel like I know well. I know him well in the way that a person's behavior tells you everything you need to know about them. Alex's journey has been chronicled in other publications though not viewed through the spiritual lens. But, when I mentioned this book to him and what its goals are, he told me of the very spiritual nature of his transition from a corporate job to his current job as owner of the Fridge gallery and event space. I got it immediately since my interactions with him up until that point had demonstrated the depths of his spiritual understanding. His loving treatment of me as a stranger made me look forward to his treatment of me as a friend. Continuing in the oral tradition, which has been the cornerstone of this book, I interviewed Alex. I had a list of nine questions, most of which I never asked. Instead, Alex shared very generously about himself, his past, his history, his family, and his life today. From what he shared and the feeling tone from which he shared I discovered his legend. We all have a legend, a story that connects the seeds of significance God has placed on the path for us to sow, a tale that reflects our choices and how those choices have impacted us and everything around us. This is Alex's.

ALEX'S STORY

Alex comes from a family that valued work. His grandmother's family was Jewish. They were refugees that had wealth at one point but lost it while his mother was still a child. Alex's mother worked from the age of seven, until well into adulthood when illness debilitated her. Alex describes his father's family as working poor. For as long as he can remember, Alex worked at various businesses for himself and others. Hard work is a family value and in his work life, Alex honored that value.

Alex is a self-described "White guy that is not quite White" due to his Jewish heritage. He says he was repeatedly reminded by others that he is Jewish when they would hear that his last name was Goldstein. Many of these reminders were accompanied by an expression of preconceived biases about Jewish people. The stereotype that Jewish people are rich and well-connected was a particular nuisance for Alex because his family did not match that stereotype.

Alex was not raised religiously though as far back as anyone remembers, everyone on both sides of Alex's family was Jewish. Being stereotyped for being Jewish shaped Alex. From the beginning he has believed in, defended, and supported the underdog. And, he has always felt a connection to a Higher Power that provided him with a sense of comfort in chaotic and painful moments, and a sense of guidance and destiny in other moments. Alex developed his spiritual understanding from exposure to Judaism, Islam, Christianity, Catholicism, and Buddhism, and from exposure to concepts like Karma.

The influence of a Higher Power is obvious in the way Alex lives his life and the serendipitous way that good fortune and misfortune have positioned him to live it.

Among Alex's gifts are design, branding, and caring. I am sure he has many others, but these are the gifts that are a part of this story. Alex graduated from Parsons School of Design in 1993. By 1998 he was well on his way to becoming an award-winning designer, working 60 and 70 hours a week and doing branding for well-known campaigns including the Do Not Call Registry. Alex has met multiple presidents and worked for government agencies in ways that have produced a global impact. For example, the branding work he did for USAID produced a brand that was awarded Global Brand of the Year. Congress mandated branding guidelines for that brand, meaning graphics Alex designed must be included on all specified items produced by the agency, on every project, everywhere in the world.

In other words, in a really short time, Alex became a noticeably big deal in the branding and graphic design world. He worked on countless projects, was extremely successful, and felt pride and pleasure in his success. But there was another side to it all. Alex was conflicted. He believed that he was living a double life. And in a sense, he was! You see, Alex was an activist, a graffiti artist, creating street art to push progressive causes. Unfortunately, the causes he forwarded during his day job often conflicted with his beliefs. The things he heard sitting in rooms with corporate and non-profit leaders and famous politicians often disturbed him. Alex made peace with these conflicts by viewing them from a spiritually empowering perspective. He understood that he had been "chosen" and that if he seriously applied himself to his purpose, what he achieved would serve the highest good.

> Alex made peace with these conflicts by viewing them from a spiritually empowering perspective. He understood that he had been "chosen" and that if he seriously applied himself to his purpose, what he achieved would serve the highest good.

Operating from this mindset, he repeatedly achieved excellence.

But the pressure on Alex intensified when his mother began to suffer the effects of Parkinson's plus, a disease that eventually took her life. Alex would drive an hour to read to his mother, after 10 or 12 hours on the job. The pressure from his mother's illness opened Alex to a deeper relationship with his Higher Power. Instead of searching for external coping mechanisms, Alex looked within. This inward-looking helped prepare him for what came next.

One day while Alex was at work, his mother died. His mother's death crushed Alex and created a rift between him and his father since his father had advised Alex to work that day. A lot of was happening and a lot of stressors were active. In the midst of it all, Alex made a decision that changed his life.

Essentially, he spoke truth to power! At an award ceremony instead of spewing the expected puffery, Alex freed his inner activist, had a mic-drop-moment, and made a political statement.

Unsurprisingly, his employer disapproved.

Alex's job instantly became a hostile place where he no longer could thrive.

Here is where you can really see Spirit's footprints. Alex had a lucrative backup plan, a plan that involved a bigger company and a more well-paying position. Alex had taken measures to ensure that upon leaving his old job he would be okay. But within weeks of taking the new job, a series of unfortunate incidents led to that job also ending. Was it a Curse or a blessing?

We all feel cursed when our dreams crumble, but sometimes, just as the butterfly is birthed from the genetic end of the caterpillar, a new, more magnificent dream is born from the end of its predecessor. That was the case with Alex! Even though he had worked only a short time on his new job when it ended, it ended with a substantial payout. This payout gave Alex room to take a breath. While taking that breath, he healed. He repaired his strained relationship with his father, which he admits took spiritual growth on his part. He began to care for his father, who had become ill. He also began to evaluate his feelings about returning to work in the design industry. Then four years after the death of Alex's mother his father died.

Alex's father bequeathed everything to Alex and Alex used his inheritance to create a meaningful legacy for his parents. Taking an incredible risk, he followed his heart, sold his parent's home, and bought and remodeled a building in an alley in DC. Now Alex lives in a part of that building and operates a community space called the Fridge in the other part.

The Fridge is the fulfillment of dreams, Alex's dreams, and the dreams of all those Alex has supported. The Fridge is a non-restricted gallery space that is inexpensive enough for those with limited finances to afford to rent.

Over 1,000 trained and untrained visual artists, some incarcerated, have had showings at the Fridge; 30 or 40 solo artists, poets, and performing artists have performed there. Weddings have been held there. Alex shares the Fridge with all the many people for whom the world has made no space. And, through the Fridge, he has changed lives and lifted people out of conditions they never thought they would be able to leave. The Fridge has changed Alex. Instead of being conflicted, he is aligned.

His True Work is to care, and he does that on the job at the Fridge and in his personal life where he mentors and supports poor and underprivileged children and teens. This is how we recognize the activity of Spirit in the outcome because Spirit is always acting to achieve the highest good for ALL. The Fridge is that good and Alex is that good!

The next champion is another of my reverend sisters. When I asked her to do this, she was attending to important personal matters, yet she made time to sit for an interview. I honor her commitment and I honor our spiritual mommas at IVISD, who through their example taught us that when God calls "yes" is the right answer. Yes, is what we do and for that, I am so grateful!

REVEREND CANDAS' STORY

When I asked about her mission Reverend Candas Ifama Barnes replied: "I am a boldly passionate collaborator. I demonstrate leadership, embody excellence, and create communities where everyone wins by engaging in daily reflective practice and committed principled action. In the end, my results are inspired, enlivened, and enlightened." Below is the story of how she came to understand her mission.

Candas spent her late teens and early twenties trying to figure out her relationship with God. Though she grew up attending church she says her relationship with God existed more because having a relationship with God is just what one did. Thus, she describes her early relationship with God as an inherited relationship, not one that was conscious, thought-out, critical, or personal. The daughter of an AME Zion Minister, Candas was raised in both her father's church and her mother's United Methodist Church. Her active participation in the church continued until she came out as a lesbian during her freshman year of college. This was the first, but not the last, time that identity played a significant role in shaping Candas' spiritual life.

Though she does not remember being told this in church, Candas picked up the message that being gay did not match with being in church. Her new lesbian identity kept her from attending church for a couple of years, but she continued to engage with God in scholarly ways, voraciously reading spiritual books, and embracing a mental path to God. Nevertheless, Candas yearned to experience more and felt shut off. She missed being in church.

At around age 22, Candas began attending a local Catholic Church with somewhat progressive views on homosexuality. Sadly, she experienced sexism within their progressive views i.e., gay men were generally accepted, lesbians much less so. During the majority of her time at the church, she had no romantic or sexual relationships with women.

Candas knew she was on a spiritual journey. She had faith. Still, she seemed unable to reconcile her relationship with God and her sexuality. So, God showed her a new Truth. She came to understand that God loved her and that her sexuality was not a mistake. Candas realized that God does not make mistakes, and she trusted that it was more important for her to authentically live the truth she believed in her heart rather than to live a lie. She again began dating women and stopped attending church.

Sometime later, Candas began attending a "gay" church with a woman who had become her partner. The yearning for a deeper relationship with God awakened within her again, causing her to attend a second church, and then a third. She went on attending three church services most Sundays and still could not discern fully what God was seeking to do through her. She sought spiritual counseling to get answers and to release her resistance to the idea of God having a call on her life. It worked! Counseling allowed her to release the resistance. The prospect of having a teaching ministry, an option introduced through counseling, piqued her interest and aligned with her desire to write and be a voice that would challenge the rabid homophobia taught in most Christian Churches at the time.

Though her relationship with God evolved and became more personal, she still had not found a theological approach that was a good fit. She attended Howard University School of Divinity for a year, and later worked and took classes at Wesley Theological Seminary. Then in 1999, after several failed relationships, bouts of depression, and other life challenges, Candas visited Inner Visions. There, she found a place that spoke peace to her Spirit and reminded her how much she longed for a spiritual community. She attended an upcoming Wonder Woman Weekend led by Reverend Doctor Iyanla Vanzant and her team, the God Squad. In the workshop, she experienced unconditional love and acceptance, unlike anything she had ever known. She became a regular volunteer for subsequent workshops and events at Inner Visions and enrolled in the inaugural class of the Inner Visions Institute for Spiritual Development (IVISD). Candas says that IVISD completely changed her life, allowed her to experience and express her gifts, and ultimately allowed her to embrace the call to ministry she had wrestled with for over a decade. There, she was also able to begin cracking the code of A Course in Miracles, which remains a foundational text in her life.

Upon ordination, Candas received the name, "Ifama," which means, "all is well." She often uses the name to remind her that all is well in moments when she experiences challenges. Candas says she now sees how nudges, impulses, and directives from Spirit invisibly guided her to where she needed to be, and to her current understanding that there is no separation between her and God—an understanding she strives to embody personally and professionally.

For over thirty years, Candas has earned the majority of her income as an American Sign Language Interpreter. She says that Divine Intervention also landed her in this profession. She had been fired from a job she hated, which led to her being hired on a temporary basis at Gallaudet, but only after the person originally assigned to the temporary position became unavailable to start due to a flat tire. The temporary position became a permanent position and led her to expand upon her passion for writing and finding ways to be a bridge for communication, an expression of the work she feels she was born for. Candas says being an interpreter has allowed her the freedom to set her own schedule, which has allowed her to pursue her calling to write. Candas already has published her first book, entitled, Sacred Musings, Volume 1: Essential Questions for Connecting Body, Mind & Spirit So You Can Live an Extraordinary Life.

> *She maintains a daily prayer practice, and she prays constantly: throughout each day, at work, and at home about work.*

Today, Candas says she has an active spiritual and devotional life replete with daily prayer and long meditative walks. She maintains a daily prayer practice, and she prays constantly: throughout each day, at work, and at home about work.

She describes herself as being in a moment-by-moment conversation with God. She describes her office as a sanctuary that includes sage, candles, an altar, the Bible, and crystals. She says she smudged it when she first started her job. And, that everyone still comments on how good the office feels. Throughout her career, Candas says she has used spiritual tools to support her in dealing with all kinds of things on the job. But in 2011, Spirit guided her through a major shutdown, when she was overcome with upset and anger after having been denied a promotion.

It is this bout of anger and upset, and what God did after it that makes Reverend Candas' story so compelling. After years of staying the path with God, years of scholarly study about God, years of living a daily devotional practice at work and home, and years of being an ordained minister; the denial of the promotion and the meaning she assigned to the denial led Candas to feel as if her center had been rocked to its core. She even announced to her supervisor that, while she would continue to do her job, she would do nothing extra, which totally was uncharacteristic.

Around this same time, Candas went through the end of the relationship with the partner she had had a commitment ceremony with only a few years before.

Depression took an even greater toll, and she began taking antidepressants.

In 2013 the combined impact of experiencing the transition of her father, a Divine nudge, and an Angela Davis speech caused a whole new Candas to emerge. She reclaimed her voice. Candas had been unhappy because she had not been selected to interpret for Angela Davis, who was to be a guest speaker at Gallaudet. Unbeknownst to Candas, this lost opportunity was a part of the Divine Design. Since she was not interpreting, Candas was free to participate. And, God had a plan! God put a question on Candas' heart, a controversial question to ask publicly in the presence of the board of trustees and the entire university. Asking such a question could have major consequences. Candas did not want to ask the question. She was at a choice point, a moment when she could either step forward in faith or fallback in fear. Candas stepped forward in faith and everything changed!

To pose God's question, Candas had to stand in all her many identities, which meant overcoming the identity challenges that previously plagued her relationship with God. When she asked the question and named her identities, Candas healed, and those who heard the question healed. By asking the question, Candas stood in Divine Identity.

In October 2018, Candas was promoted to a newly created position, Manager of Intercultural Competency Development and Campus Climate. In that role, she embraced the aspect of her work as a voice for the voiceless and a bold and passionate communicator. To get to this point, Candas says she had to grow. After the upset over the lost promotion, Candas examined herself and acknowledged that she was not being 100% responsible for her experience at work; instead, she had been deflecting, blaming, and projecting. She put support systems in place and became less reactive and more responsible and intentional. She sets goals around what she wanted to create, and she consciously attempted to become the change she wished to experience. Candas now takes full ownership of her outcomes on the job.

During the spring of 2019, she realized that while the new position she had taken was important, she and it were not the right fit for one another. She resigned and returned to her career as an interpreter knowing that clarity about her next most appropriate steps was being revealed.

As she continues on the path of flowing into the next expression of her Divine Identity, Candas shows up body, mind, and spirit at work. She regularly follows Spirit's urgings and has become known for her outspoken willingness to take a stand. This she does with an understanding of the risk she is taking and an appreciation for her privileged position of eldership and seniority that allows her some protection. Candas understands that speaking out is a part of her True Work, and she has sought additional training to become more effective at it. Now, when she speaks, her constant intention is to do so in ways that ensure that her words are heard and received, and, that she always leaves those listening, whole.

Candas says she now pays more attention to the nudges and the still small voice and chooses what feels good. In her experience, what feels good also serves the highest good. She believes that God wants ease and grace for all of us, not struggle, effort, and opposition. And she believes that when we choose to struggle, we are doing a disservice to our Higher Self.

Currently, Candas is undergoing a physical body transformation that she says also is God-ordained. She has built a business around it. It is a part of the newness that God is calling her toward at work and home. She says that she has learned not just to hold on to something because she chose it at some time in the past. Instead, through her ongoing conversation with Spirit, she is constantly in a state of discovery, constantly in the question of what feels good and right. When it is time to choose again, she says with gratitude, and, an understanding of lessons learned, she releases what has served its purpose.

The final story also is about a former coaching client. Her story is one of extreme transformation. I interviewed her for this book and tried to capture it all in words. Still, I am not sure that what I have written conveys the feeling tone of what transpired. The best I can say is that once again God showed up and showed out. It is breathtaking! This is Linda's story.

LINDA'S STORY

For as long as she remembers, Linda has believed in the existence of a Higher Being, whom she refers to as God. Linda, like Alex, was not raised to follow tenets of a particular religion, but she was raised to pray. She can remember praying from the time she was a very little girl. Linda's family prayed, and she followed their example. But there was also a darker side to Linda's family. Physical and sexual abuse was the norm in her family. From the age of six years old, Linda's prayer was, "Dear God, please take me from this home."

At age 12, God answered the prayer. Linda was removed from her home. Linda's faith in God and determination to change her life grew.

> *Undeniably, and with unbelievable momentum, Linda transformed pain into progress!*

I continued to be amazed at the power of Linda's story and how she has overcome and reconciled the challenges of her birth family. When we met and decided to work together, I knew a large part of the work would center around purifying and transmuting emotional pain, so that Linda could profit from her life experiences and move forward. The first part of our work together began that process. And God was in the work. I felt the Presence, and Linda says she felt it too. She felt drawn to continue coaching. And, she continued against the advice of her psychotherapist, who unbeknownst to me, disagreed with the method I employed to support Linda in transcending pain. Undeniably, and with unbelievable momentum, Linda transformed pain into progress!

She reports that from the very first exercise, she was able to discern that God was present and operating to carry her through each painful experience. And, because coaching is a collaborative growth experience, my faith, confidence, and power grew, along with Linda's. In other words, God taught us both using Linda's life experiences. So powerful is the healing in Linda's story, her transparency in sharing it, and, the good she manifests from it;

that an entire book could be written about her transformation. I hope she will inspire others by one day authoring that book.

Before our coaching work, Linda's gods (with a small "g") had been effort and excellence. When God answered her prayer and removed her from her birth home, Linda applied effort and excellence to manage the experience. She believed that all of the success in her life could be attributed to effort and excellence. So, it is no surprise that Linda considered her work to have become her identity. At that point, she believed herself to be nothing without her job as an assistant principal. Linda believed her job was the fulfillment of her childhood dream to become a success and support her family. Linda happily worked from sunup to sundown often not arriving home until 10 p.m. From her efforts, she expected reward and progression because her effort and excellence had always led to the accomplishment of her goals.

> *Being passed over toppled the gods of effort and excellence Linda had believed in.*

Then, the unthinkable happened! Linda, who had worked with the founder in founding the school; Linda, who everyone had said was the obvious choice, was passed over for promotion to principal. Being passed over toppled the gods of effort and excellence Linda had believed in.

Despite her having expended extreme effort and delivered extreme excellence, the bosses had overlooked her. To add insult to injury, Linda was directed to aid the newly-appointed principal. She was to teach him how to run the school that she loved, already understood, and was more than qualified to lead. Linda was frustrated, angry, and confused. She did not realize God was calling her to fulfill a new destiny.

Linda remembers being asked in one of our coaching sessions: "What makes you think you were supposed to get that job?" She says the question infuriated and insulted her; but also, it sat with her and awakened something. Linda says it opened her up to the truth of her job, the truth of her family life, the truth of her friendships. The truth was that if she would only say "no" to less, she could get more of what she was deserved. Linda used the *question to propel herself into Divine Identity, effectively using her yes's and no's to answer the question, who am I?*

Linda says that through coaching, she started to feel good and believe in herself. The prayers in the coaching sessions amplified her natural love of prayer. She would wake up praying, pray throughout the school day, and pray at home. And with her prayers, things intensified.

As sometimes happens, things got worse before they got better. This is worth understanding! God grows us into the positions we are to be in. Healing is growing. We have a broad universe of concern: all the things we care about, desire, worry over or have no clue about that concern us. Within this universe, we have a narrow radius of control, narrower than we would care to admit, which includes the few things we can act on (not determine the outcome of). When we connect with God and act on the things within our radius of control, God aligns with our actions. God then addresses the other aspects of our universe of concern, those other things over which we have no direct influence. This is why Jesus in John 5:17 speaks of His Father's work and His own work. We act and God acts. When we take connected action, God meets us where we are.

Now, depending on where we are, the beginning and middle of "God meeting us" can look and feel crazy. That was the case for Linda! Things intensified at school. She was assaulted by the new male principal and a lawsuit was in the works. Yet, through it all, Linda continued praying and growing.

> *All this is to say that to have the life we want we must become fertile ground for that life.*

Life experiences are governed by consciousness. We can only say "yes" to as much as we can handle. Our experiences can be reduced to the ideas that gave birth to them.

Likewise, our strongly held ideas eventually manifest and reflect in our experiences.

All this is to say that to have the life we want we must become fertile ground for that life.

Fertile ground is a consciousness where beautiful ideas about yourself and your life are held, fed, nurtured, projected, and allowed to manifest into stable, positive experiences. Without this state of consciousness, good is produced, but not sustained; it is temporary good, built on shifting sand (Matthew 7:24-27). When doubt, unworthiness, and not-good-enough appear; when fear appears, or anger and trouble disrupt, temporary good collapses.

> Linda says that what she gained in coaching was a new kind of education that allowed her to live a new kind of brilliance.

Linda was faithful in connecting. God grew her into her good so that the consciousness that she projected it from became fertile ground, a firm rock that could withstand the wind, the rain, and the rivers of change. Linda was steadfast! She continued to pray! She did not settle and say "yes" to less. She gave her full self to God, and she received God's full self. God ignited Linda's capacities and faculties. Linda reports that her heart opened wide. She began to vibrate with the energy of "all is well." And all became well! The lawsuit became unnecessary. The school removed the principal. A new opportunity was delivered and dropped at her feet without effort on her part.

Linda says that what she gained in coaching was a new kind of education that allowed her to live a new kind of brilliance.

She learned how to align with what she desired, how to grow toward it, and how to allow it to come forth. Linda honors this as a distinctive way of being in the world and she brings it to those she works with.

Through God, Linda's territories have expanded! You see, Linda's destiny was beyond the job of principal. Only after she released her desire and upset over not getting that job could she grow into the destiny God had prepared her for.

Now, Linda is creating a safe culture and climate across all the schools in the New York boroughs by overseeing the implementation of restorative justice practices. These practices allow children, families, teachers, and *even administrative stakeholders to build community, and prevent and repair harm through social-emotional learning. Linda's experiences in her birth family uniquely qualify her to bring deep empathy to this work. She is happy, relaxed, and well-loved by those she works with and supervises. While once she worried about crossing t's and dotting i's for fear of appearing deficient, Linda now reports that she feels like she is working with family. For the first time, she works on a first-name basis, collaboratively and cooperatively with those she supervises. Linda says God opened her to the truth that it is not about being the boss; it is about growing together. She says she learns from those she works with, just as they learn from her. And, she says her staff requests her supervisory feedback sessions because each session begins with connection and support, energy that elevates the work they are doing for children, families, and schools.*

Linda is doing her True Work! Still, she misses connecting with children and longs for an opportunity to share directly with children the things she has learned and the ways she has grown. God is awakening a new itch in Linda, and as with us all, the story of her True Work remains unfinished. I am excited to see what happens next!

Sensei Subira: Reverend Kelli, are there common threads in the stories that we can identify to sum things up?

Reverend Kelli: Here are a few that I see.

- Know yourself at home and work.
- Love! Work does not have to be a love-free zone.
- Be courageous and do that which scares you.
- Confront the truth, it may hurt, but, it grows you.
- Demonstrate faith and do not give up in the middle.
- Act. It is through action that you receive God's feedback.
- Do not settle. Settling is just another form of giving up.
- Follow Spirit's lead.
- Pay attention as the lessons unfold.
- The path may wind through rocky territory.
- Do not try to figure things out.

- Practice perfects.
- God's timing is perfect.
- Commit! Dare! Serve!

Serve! That is the one though! There is something about service that ignites and inspires. One of the best ways we can serve is to do our True Work, our heart work, and all work from a stance of deep compassion and committed love. That is the stuff of champions!

Champions Do not Retreat; They Grow, Face, and Forward Environments around Them, As They Make Themselves Centers of Good.

Chapter

Stop Dying to Make a Living: Choose Divinity, Not Karoshi

To gain that which is worth having, it may be necessary to lose everything else.

~ Bernadette Devlin ~

The price of dishonesty is self-destruction.

~ Rita Mae Brown ~

We have free will, but our free will lies in our choice of thoughts.

~ Emmet Fox ~

Living life in alignment with our Divine identity can be a daily challenge. On the job, the high cost of achieving alignment may tempt us to default to one of many false ego identities. Below we discuss how settling for the false may come at a deadly cost, figuratively and literally. This chapter is about how important it is to make Divine identity your refuge.

Sensei Subira: Reverend Kelli, you believe that embracing Divine identity on the job is not just a luxury that can elevate our success on the job; you believe it is a matter of life and death. Tell us more about identity and Divine alignment on the job.

Alignment makes you more powerful, influential, and valuable.

Reverend Kelli: Let me talk about what I see as the good news first. I see success on the job as flowing from embracing Divine identity, not from abandoning it in favor of false ego-born identities. If you are willing to work from the heart and be present to the people you encounter, if you are willing to relax allegiance to rules and policies, and amplify empathy, love, and understanding; there is a massive opportunity for you to experience satisfaction and fulfillment on the job.

I am talking about connecting with God within you and knowing and connecting with that same God within the people on the job. I am talking about doing what is needed, not merely what is commonly done. I am not talking about rebelling against your employer. I am talking about being bigger than your job, doing more, loving harder. That is it!

I am talking about being responsible, able to respond, and accountable, the one with whom the buck stops, for the experience you and others have on the job. When you are willing to step outside of the common framework and use creative problem solving and your own judgment, and willing to be accountable for any penalties you experience, (because there may be penalties), then you will possess the keys to open a positive Pandora's box of possibilities. Everything at work will gel, guide you down the spiritual path, show you delicious lessons, and be fodder for your joyful growth and the elevation of the environment around you. Alignment makes you more powerful, influential, and valuable.

When you are aligned with Spirit you bring Divinely inspired creative thoughts to the workplace. Then your contribution creates opportunities for advancement. Ask yourself, if you had automaton number one, two, three, four, and five on the one hand, and a Divinely connected, creative being on the other, who would you promote? When you are aligned, you shine by having stepped out of the mold, the framework of lockstep that everyone is in. Without Divine connection, people are missing the opportunity to stand out and be seen, because they are trying too hard to fit in.

Sensei Subira: That is clear. I get the benefits of Divine connection. Now, let us talk about the other side. Discuss the consequences or the dangers of working on the job without Divine alignment.

Reverend Kelli: Work-related suicide is the gravest consequence. It is the consequence that inspired me to write this chapter and the consequence that I want readers to avoid. Too often, work-related suicide is downplayed because suicide itself is taboo. I often work on projects located in downtown offices. On three occasions, I have been at work and had a suicide occur where a person jumped from a building near my workplace. One of the people who jumped was a lawyer, and I suspect at least one of the other two also was a lawyer, so this trend caught my attention.

Dissatisfaction in the workplace can feel devastating. What I imagine happens is that a person has tied their identity to their job. Whether it is a corporation or law firm or whatever the job, it has become everything. They have spent 60, 70, 80, and maybe even 100 hours a week on the job and have sacrificed their lives for it. Maybe they did not see their kids as often as they would have or maybe they even chose not to have kids. Or, as was the case with me, maybe their marriage fell apart because they did not give enough attention to it. When a person has made all these sacrifices, and then something happens with the job where they find themselves unable to keep up, or the job does not want them anymore, or they become aware that the job is not worthy of the sacrifice, it implodes and suicide becomes a way out.

> *Work hard, but plug into the right source of energy, that source being Spirit.*

In Japan, work-related suicide is so prevalent it has a name. The Japanese call it *Karoshi*, and it not only includes work-related suicides; it includes people who very literally work themselves to death. In Japan, there are 24 and 25-year-olds having heart attacks and strokes because they are working so hard.

I believe in hard work. Work hard, but plug into the right source of energy, that source being Spirit.

When you are plugged into Spirit, you can stand in your identity without sacrificing your mental and physical health, regardless of what people around you may be doing. Some people in Japan, reportedly, have starved themselves to death, working so hard literally they were dying from not eating.

Sensei Subira: That is frightening!

Reverend Kelli: Exactly! This is such a pressing issue, especially in the legal profession, that the January/February 2019 edition of the *Washington Lawyer* addressed the impact of workloads and other work-related pressures on judges and lawyers. For me, one of the most significant causes they discussed, in addition to the things you might imagine like heavy workloads, stress, and harassment, was something they referred to as vicarious trauma. This concept is so interesting. I think it applies across the board, not just to judges and lawyers.

Our empathic connection to one another is so profound that we are naturally impacted by the traumatic suffering of others whom we encounter on and off the job. Trauma leaks from the lives of those around us and can have a corrosive effect on all levels of our being: mental, physical, emotional, spiritual, and energetic. This is particularly true where the trauma is caused by us, even if we are acting as a proxy for our job.

Divine connection offsets the pain of this kind of incongruence. It cleanses and reenergizes. It allows us to stand with clarity and strength and to know the truth of our innocence and safety. It quells fears and relaxes frustration and stress. Without Divine connection, relief may be available through therapy of other secular stress-relievers, but unfortunately, so many times people do not seek help, because they have a belief that they have to be strong.

Instead of positive stress-relievers, people choose negative forms of stress abatement such as consuming junk food, alcohol, drugs, and other harmful substances. And, when long work hours, depression, missed sleep, relationship problems, or finances continue to weigh on them, they fold and fold hard. For example, according to a *Washington Lawyer* article, a study of 13,000 practicing lawyers showed that 21% to 36% of them reported drinking problems. Courthouses are responding to the toxicity of the legal workplace by implementing stress relief programs including mindfulness programs. Even in courthouses which I consider to be the most secular of secular arenas, spiritual techniques are being deployed.

Sensei Subira: I remember the It Gets Better Campaign, formed to respond to bullying and suicide of LGBTQ kids. How is the rest of the US population doing?

Reverend Kelli: It is terrible in many sectors. According to the US Department of Veterans Affairs, each day about 20 veterans commit suicide. The suicide rate for veterans and active-duty service members is reportedly 50% higher than for civilians. Firefighters and police officers also have elevated rates of suicide. *USA Today* reported 103 firefighters and 140 police officers died by suicide in 2017, while 93 firefighters and 129 police officers died in the line of duty. Citing BLUE H.E.L.P. and FBHA, the March 11, 2020 article, "More First Responders Dying by Suicide than in Line of Duty" reported even larger numbers for 2019. According to the article, in 2019 there were 133 reported firefighter suicides and 228 reported police officer suicides.[16]

Karoshi means death from overwork.

Sensei Subira: So, more firefighters and police officers died from suicide than in the line of duty?

Reverend Kelli: That is right. The NIH National Institute of Mental Health, (citing the Centers for Disease Control and Prevention WISQARS Leading Causes of Death Reports for 2018) reports that in 2018 suicide was the 10th-leading cause of death in the United States claiming 48,344 lives (two and a half times the 18, 830 people, who died by homicide). In that same year suicide was the second-leading cause of death among people ages 10 to 34 and the fourth-leading cause among people ages 35 to 54.[17] Between 2007 and 2018, the national suicide rate among persons aged 10–24 increased by 57.4%. The increase was not limited to one region or state. It was the result of an increase in youth suicides in a majority of states.[18] I believe that right here in America we are suffering from a subtle form of *Karoshi*.[19]

Sensei Subira: We are throwing around this word *Karoshi*. What exactly does *Karoshi* mean?

Reverend Kelli: Karoshi means death from overwork.

But for our purposes, I would like to refine that definition to death from overstress. Without even accounting for unique stressors in an individual's life there are universal stressors that impact all of us, the threat of climate crisis, the impact of aging, the experience of societal politics, and now the global Covid-19 pandemic. And, how about the speed of change! Knowledge is said to be doubling about every 13 months, and it is moving toward doubling every 12 hours. This creates stress because when knowledge moves fast, change moves fast, and we feel the pressure of that speed. And now, many also face the stress of virtual learning, virtual teaching, remote working, and isolation from family and friends. Even Facebook and Instagram add pressure: the pressure of being connected to others, comparing, and contrasting, tied into their successes and failures, sadness, and joy, trying to support them. This is vicarious trauma.

Divine Self is the place from which all of this, all of life must be answered. Divine Self anchors identity in a world that strips identity away.

Spiritual practice releases pressure. No matter what the job, the pressure needs release—the pressure of working harder, longer, faster, of incorporating more and more knowledge and information, and of adapting to more and more change in the workplace. This particularly applies to the pressures caused by areas of incongruity—where the rules, policies, outcomes, and behaviors on the job conflict with who you are and who you want to be.

Sensei Subira: Does our work ethic also give rise to pressure?

Reverend Kelli: Work ethic is part of it, both individual work ethic and cultural work ethic. In the US, we live in a culture of mottos that extol the value of hard work, of pulling oneself up by one's bootstraps, rugged individualism, and so on. The work of Malcolm Gladwell and others who have looked at the issue suggests these mottos are more myth than legend.

Sensei Subira: Meaning?

Reverend Kelli: Meaning, they reflect more what we would like to have been true about us than what is historically accurate. Privilege, the cheating scandal, the Wall Street bailout, the prison pipeline, corporate tax breaks that result in zero taxes paid by wealthy corporations, preferences for the wealthy, and slavery itself, put the lie to these mottos.

Sensei Subira: Yes, slavery! You have some unique views about that. Would you share them?

Reverend Kelli: We are stepping a bit off track but okay we can explore a bit. I will start with a book called *The Half Has Never Been Told: Slavery and the Making of American Capitalism,* written by fellow Georgetown alum, Edward Baptist.[20] This book should be required reading for every American. I would love to see even a simplified summarized version offered for young kids. It provides an in-depth look at the system of slavery, the business of slavery, and how that business propelled this country into superpower status. It explains the quota expectation for each slave, and how that expectation consistently increased with physical punishment as the consequence for failing to hit the quota. This meant that those who were enslaved had to learn to place craft above calling. In other words, they had to become good at the craft they were forced to do, rather than being able to obey their calling and do their heart's desire. This emphasis on craft over calling continues to be a feature of capitalism today.

> *Emphasis on craft over calling continues to be a feature of capitalism today.*

Similarly, capitalism, at least since the time of slavery, has put profits above ethical and spiritual alignment. Am I saying that capitalism is inherently unethical? No. I am saying that the free market is not naturally predisposed to consider ethics and spiritual alignment. Thus, it is for us to consider them and infuse them in the way we individually and collectively choose to live within our capitalist system.

In my opinion, the system of slavery and all that the slavers came to learn from it informs and underpins employer-employee relationships. It has throughout our history as a nation, and in many ways today it still does. It also has been a protocol we have exported globally. We could not help but export it, because it is interwoven in the version of capitalism we exported.

Sensei Subira: Now, I have heard you talk about the spiritual reason for slavery. Do you want to talk about that or save it for another time?

Reverend Kelli: Sensei, I think that is a whole other book! Did you know that the life expectancy for an enslaved person working on a sugar plantation was seven years! I learned that at the National Museum of African American History and Culture.[21] The so-called cooperation of Africans with the slave trade was often to avoid the enslavement of their own tribe, and because American slavery was uniquely barbaric in the history of world slavery, they had little idea of the heinous experience they were dooming their countrymen to endure.

Sensei Subira: I have always wondered, why do you think people even believe it matters whether some Africans aided in the slave trade?

Reverend Kelli: Well, this is not an exact fit, but I liken it to the people who talk about the parents who allowed their children to hang out with R Kelly or Michael Jackson or others who have been accused of abuse. It is sort of a belief that if the parent, who had a superior duty to ensure the safety and well-being of the abused person, neglected that duty, then the culpability of the abuser is mitigated. Its logical foundation is two wrongs CAN make a right. But they cannot! The involvement of Africans in the slave trade is irrelevant to me and does not at all excuse what happened once the kidnapped people arrived on American soil. If anything mitigates the actions of the slavers, which I question whether anything about their action is mitigable, it was the mindset with which they were afflicted. None of us can rise above our mindset without Divine intervention, grace, and growth.

Sensei Subira: I love the way you compare slavery to child abuse.

Reverend Kelli: I know it is like comparing apples and tomatoes, but hey, they are both red fruits!

What I truly mean is that if certain truths were told about slavery, Blacks in this country would swell with pride over the accomplishments, sacrifices, and resilience of our enslaved ancestors. Those men, women, and children endured hell so this country could rise to its destiny. They are to be celebrated like the great soldiers of any war. They are to be studied for their ability to rise above and thrive through the deplorable conditions of slavery. They are among the true heroes of America's story.

We all owe them an incalculable debt.

Sensei Subira: Amen to that, Sis!

Reverend Kelli: Now let me bring this full circle and come back to the choice between Divinity and *Karoshi*.

In my opinion, no people on earth throughout history have more clearly lived and worked this choice than those who experienced slavery; those, like the workers on the sugar plantations, who were worked to death; those who sang spirituals and turned to God and one another for relief.

When I hear Black people talk about employers and what is required of them on the job, in this conversation, I often hear a declaration: "I am not their slave!" or, "They are trying to treat me like their slave." I even may have said it myself in moments of frustration. But, in my heart, I know our enslaved ancestors are to be admired, not negated. Their ability to rise above working conditions and survive through tenacity, the sheer will to live, and Divine connection, is to be emulated. The mystical purpose of their presence in this country continues to unfold through us all. We honor it when we choose to live out our Divine purpose on the job.

Karoshi, death from overwork, death from over-stress, happens on the physical level; and it also can happen on the spiritual level. I am talking about the death of purpose. You choose *Karoshi* when you identify with the job so deeply and completely that you and your job become, *we*; and you simultaneously abandon your, *I*, the fulfillment of your True Work, and the *I AM* seeking to express through you. You commit suicide; maybe not a physical suicide (though as statistics have shown, it could turn to that), but a smothering of your Divine Self. I do not think there is anything you can do to kill your Divine Self, even physical suicide, but you certainly can put it into a deep, deep sleep and set yourself up for a spiritual wake-up call. And as you know, Sensei, these can be pretty unpleasant!

Sensei Subira: Yes, I think we have all gotten that spiritual boot in the butt!

Reverend Kelli: I know I have, and I have still got the boot-print to prove it!

Sensei Subira: So, the bottom line is that folks should make a choice, not just do nothing and hope for the best?

Reverend Kelli: Well, you know the lyrics of that old Burt Bacharach song:

"Wishin' and hopin' and thinkin' and prayin'

Plannin' and dreamin' each night of his charms,

That won't get you into his arms." [22]

Maybe praying will; but the point is, do not default into a way of being. Choose! And, when the choice has been made to align with Divinity (I am assuming no one reading this book would choose *Karoshi* consciously), then do the work it takes to manifest the fruits of that choice!

Choose God Now. Ignite Sacred Unfolding.
God Is Life. True Work Is Life-giving.

Book II

THEN

101 Simple Coaching Tips to Ascend Beyond Challenges in Your Workplace

People pay for what they do, and still more for what they have allowed themselves to become. And they pay for it very simply; by the lives they lead.

~ James Baldwin ~

By choosing we learn to be responsible. By paying the price of our choices we learn to make better choices.

~ Marsha Sinetar ~

Judge your success by what you had to give up to get it.

~ Dalai Lama ~

Trying to fit into an employer's culture can feel artificial and uncomfortable. It can even cause you to question whether the job you are in is the right job for you. I understand this. Of course, you want to be yourself and still succeed in your job. You probably know that you cannot treat your job like it is a frat house. You probably know how important it is to behave like a professional; still, professional expectations can be a bit tricky and paradoxical.

In Book I, NOW, I offered the spiritual rules of the road. In Book II, THEN, I take another approach. I offer practical advice to support you while you use spiritual practices to manifest a new job or a new experience at your job. While I could not create coaching tips that perfectly fit every workplace, I have created a template of tips that I know you can adapt to fit your workplace perfectly. I have faith in God and faith in you. And remember, I am only an email away!

I named this second book "THEN" because it outlines an approach that draws from who I was before spiritual authenticity was my priority. I have massaged these tips to add light. However, if any tip is out of alignment with your spiritual worldview, I encourage you to defer to Spirit. These tips are not theoretical; they are drawn from actual experiences. If you choose to apply them, I hope that they support you in adapting to life at your job, while you practice spirituality at work.

Tip No. 1

Be Kind to All Always.

Do not be nasty or snarky, even if you think the person is on a low level and cannot impact your position. Energetically, everything matters. If you want to receive positive energy, give positive energy. No one is impressed by nastiness. It may be tempting to pass on the nasty if someone has been nasty to you. Or you may want to emulate a mentor or other firm superstar who is known for nastiness. But, trust me when I tell you, their superstardom is the reason their nastiness is tolerated; it is not the cause of their superstardom. Rumors spread. If you are nasty, it will not be long before you have a reputation, and being nasty is not a reputation you want. If you cannot help yourself, exercise more to release the angry energies. Try to get to the bottom of what has you on edge and process it. Work your spiritual practice until you find a way to resolve the nasty energy.

Tip No. 2

Have a Good Handshake.

Problem handshakes are a regular complaint I have heard from interviewers. Again, it seems insignificant, but many folks believe it to be very telling. So, even if you have read about fancy handshakes in work success books, I advise you to stay as far away from these ploys as possible. A simple handshake conveys a simple message, "I know how to shake hands, and my handshake is not the most noteworthy thing about me."

Do not shake hands with a super-firm handshake. Shaking hands is not a strength contest. Your job is not to shake the other person into submission. Do not make your handshake a power play. Doing so is transparent and unappreciated by most, who are on the receiving end of the shake. If you do not know your strength, and cannot figure out the appropriate level of pressure, practice with a friend.

Also, do not shake hands with a limp handshake, a wet handshake, or a handshake that uses the other hand as a closer; instead, think a pleasant thought, such as, I like you, I would love to do business with you, or, you have a great reputation. Then, make eye contact with the other person, look sincere, smile, and send positive energy.

Tip No. 3

Be Careful with Credit Cards.

If the company provides a credit card for business purposes, use it carefully. Companies often provide employees with a credit card intended for business use. For many employees, this credit card becomes a source of trouble. Five primary problems arise. First, where the company allows personal use of the card, employees often overspend, overextending the card on personal items and not leaving enough of a credit line to pay for the business items for which they are expected to pay. Do not use the card for personal purposes. Second, employees use the card on personal items that are inappropriate, giving the firm a window into their personal lives that reflects poorly on them. Third, employees spend on the card at times and places that are contrary to where they are supposed to be and what they are supposed to be doing or simply in inappropriate places. Fourth, employees do a poor job understanding their company's rules governing allowable business expenses and purchase expensive items that the company will not reimburse. Fifth, employees do a poor job of record-keeping and have no way tying expenses to the appropriate clients.

Tip No. 4

Use the Magic Formula.

This technique is invaluable in situations where you are being assigned projects you cannot or do not want to do. By and large, those with the authority to assign projects expect that you will accept whatever it is they assign you. It is important that you be viewed as a person who will do exactly that, who will accept whatever work is assigned to you. Ultimately, over the long term, you will end up being assigned projects and doing projects you would have preferred not to do. This technique is for those other times, the times when you absolutely cannot bring yourself to do what is being asked of you. Warning: do not overuse this technique, or sooner or later, people will catch on to the fact that you are cherry-picking projects.

So here it is, never say "no" to work; say "yes" with great enthusiasm! Call it, the "yes-and" approach. It works like this. When the assignment is made, say "yes," agree to do it, be excited about it. Then, before the person assigning the matter begins to explain the details, add an "and." The "and" will be a lead-in to all the conditions that must first be met before you can take on the project. For example, "Yes, I can take on the project, and, I will need to do x first," or, "Yes, I will take on the project, and I will have to check with y (some other person who assigns you projects) about x (some other project you have been assigned) to determine my timeline for completing it."

The contingencies ideally should be actual barriers or obstacles that stand in the way of you taking on the new project.

So, to use this process, honestly evaluate the reasons you cannot or do not want to take on the project. Choose the barriers that are the most valid, job-related reasons. Practice using the "yes-and" approach with a family member or friend in a non-work-related context. The goal is to become very proficient in its use before you need to use it. If you are not good at using the approach and attempt to use it, your efforts will be transparent; and to the assignor, it may appear as if you are simply avoiding work.

Tip No. 5

Be an Effective Timekeeper.

Make sure you have a good understanding of the company's timekeeping practices. If you do not work in an environment where your time is tracked, this can be as simple as knowing the rules on timely arrival, breaks, lunch, and departure. If you do work in an environment where time is tracked, it means you must know how entries are supposed to be written. For example, when recording a phone call, should the names of the participants be listed? If multiple company employees are participating in a phone call, each should agree upon the amount of time spent on the call; otherwise, rounding up or down can make time entries appear to be inaccurate. Do not shave hours to make yourself look faster than you are.

Remember, for companies that require timekeeping, such as law firms, accounting firms, and government contractors, any perceived errors in timekeeping can interfere with the company's profits. Some clients may even look for a reason to dispute items on a bill to avoid paying or to reduce fees.

Know your client! Some clients do not like being charged for phone calls. Others do not like being charged for inter-company meetings. Many will scrutinize the amount of time it takes to write a letter or the number of people involved in the process of writing it. The assignor likely will know the idiosyncrasies of the client. Check with them and see if there is anything special you need to know.

Do not steal time, and do not give it away. Be accurate. Fudging time is noticed. Even if no one mentions it, trust that they are aware of it. When or if a rumor spreads that you are fudging time, some may see you as lazy or incompetent, or worse, as a cheat. If you work for a job that requires timekeeping, learn proper timekeeping narratives, and follow them tightly. Again, the person in charge will have the inside information on timekeeping for the project. Confer with him or her and abide by what you are told. Be informed of the standards in advance and then apply the information provided.

Tip No. 6

Do Not Send Organization-wide Emails.

Unless doing so is a routine part of your job responsibilities, do not send organization-wide emails. Even if you receive prior permission to send such an email, in doing so you are bound to ruffle someone's feathers. The most benign communications irritate the irritable and busy. It is a no-win proposition. If the email is insignificant, it is damned for its insignificance. It gives rise to the question, why was it necessary to send out this insignificant email to the entire firm? If it is significant, then someone is bound to disagree with its content and oppose it and you for that reason. It may seem insignificant to you, but it may seem significant to someone within your organization. I know of a young woman, who was fired after two of these organization-wide emails. Of course, the emails were not given as the reason for the firing. The emails were viewed as further evidence that the woman had bad judgment and was a bad fit. The emails caused people to pay attention to her in a negative way. You do not want negative attention.

This is not an instance where any attention is good attention. Thousands of brilliant, hardworking people cycle through corporations every year. You do not get through the door without the smarts. Those who do not choose to work hard usually leave. Those who stay, endeavor to fit. This term, *fit*, is an all-encompassing one that describes one's ability to meet the range of corporate cultural expectations. Some think *fit* is just a dog whistle for racism, sexism, homophobia, and the like, but it is more nuanced than that. Corporations work hard to create a corporate identity, and they want their employees to embody that identity. They want employees who will eagerly conform to the company's "we" and those who cannot or will not are viewed as a problem, as a bad fit. Bad fits do not last long, unless what they bring to the corporation is irreplaceable, and then only while the thing they bring remains of value.

The best way of handling an organization-wide email is to get someone else (someone whose job typically includes sending out organization-wide emails) to do it for you.

Tip No. 7

Limit Personal Phone Calls.

Limit personal phone calls, in terms of length and frequency. You may think that no one is paying attention; but, people pay far more attention than you realize. Behave as if someone is watching because they usually are. This advice is even more critical if you are making and receiving personal calls on a work phone answered by a secretary or receptionist, or if you are using a cell phone provided by your job. Within a company, people talk. Part of my current job involves reading thousands of internal company emails. Believe me, everything you think people do not notice or talk about, they do. So, do not give them anything to talk about. Keep your personal life personal.

Tip No. 8

Keep Your Side Business *Your* Business.

Backchannel talk often ruins careers.

Many of us dream of owning our own business. This may be your dream. Or, you simply may want or need a bit of extra income to help make ends meet. Your job may seem like fertile ground for promoting or marketing your business. Colleagues and co-workers may even encourage you. Unfortunately, this is another troublesome area. While people may be encouraging when your business is in its nascent stages, the more significant it becomes, and the more serious you become about it, the more of a problem it will become for you at work. The scary part is that you may not even know it is a problem. Backchannel talk often ruins careers.

A little bit of buzz into the wrong ears about you and your business and next, people are wondering about your loyalties, questioning your whereabouts, and questioning your use of firm resources, whether you may be misappropriating them for use in your own business. In my work as a consultant reviewing employee disciplinary issues, I have seen this. And, I have heard about it when coaching clients.

No amount of honesty will stem the tide of rumors once they begin. The best way to stop rumors is to prevent them from starting. Keep your side business *your* business.

Tip No. 9

Do Not Bring Your Kids to Work.

No matter how well-behaved or charming your kids are, unless you are the boss, getting a reputation for bringing your children to work will not help your career prospects. Do you work at a daycare center, a pre-school, as

Have childcare and backup childcare in place.

a kid's sports coach, or in some other field that involves children or young people? If so, it is probably okay for you to bring your kids to your job, if that aligns with the culture at your job. If you do not work at one of these places, it is probably not okay.

It is natural to want to mix your home life and your life on the job. You are likely proud of your children and would like to show them off to the people you work with, or at least to let the people you work with connect a face to stories about your children you have told. You may think it is important for your children to see the place that you go to every day and for them to have a sense of what you do. You may even think that taking your children to work will reinforce your child's work ethic or sense of the value of money. Maybe, you believe that bringing your kids around will remind your job that you have kids and subconsciously cause them to allow you more time for your family. Or, maybe you may want to show your job that you are a family man or woman. I get it!

Most workplaces have events where people are allowed and encouraged to bring the family—this is the right time to bring your children. Have childcare and backup childcare in place.

If necessary, take a sick day to take care of your children, or work from home if you have access.

Even if you are the boss, before choosing to bring your children to work, you may want to consider the example you are setting for your employees. Are you willing to allow them to bring their kids to the job? Are you willing to flaunt a privilege you are willing to extend to the people who work for you?

Tip No. 10

Be Punctual.

Arrive at meetings on time and arrive at your job each morning on time. Yes, everyone has emergencies occasionally. Here, I am discussing your routine. If there is a good reason you regularly must arrive late or toward the back end of what is acceptable, make sure the rumor mill knows why. Arriving on time or early demonstrates a certain seriousness that employers look for. Again, if you are a salaried employee, no one is likely to comment directly, but that does not mean it is not being discussed.

I once worked with a person who left her suit jacket on the back of her chair. This person arrived late and left early regularly. She seemed to believe a suit jacket on a chair would convince people that she was in the office. It did not. She was judged for "working banker hours" and for the jacket on the chair. For this and other reasons, she was placed "on the radar," and being on the radar never goes well. Everything she did was scrutinized, and, ultimately, she was terminated.

Tip No. 11

No Shouting.

If your job is to work as a sports coach or a trader on Wall Street, yes, you may be expected to shout. If you do not work in a job like that, you are expected NOT to shout. It is probably obvious that you should not shout at another company employee, whether they sit under, above, or beside you in the pecking order. But, also avoid shouting at an adversary, competitor, family member, or friend. When on the job, avoid shouting even to yourself. Like the tantrums of a child, the shouting of an adult on the job signifies immaturity.

No matter how much temporary success angry antics get you, they are not worth it because of the permanent harm such antics do to your reputation and energy. In the long run, the old saying is true: you will attract more flies with honey than you will with vinegar.

Tip No. 12

No Crying.

Yes, there probably will be events that just make you want to cry on the job. When inconsistencies and incongruence scrape against who you are, when people upset or frustrate you, when the stressors make you feel overwhelmed, tears are natural. And, a lone tear rolling down your cheek will not bring the world to an end. Still, as a rule, crying in a location where anyone else can see or hear you is to be avoided.

Whether you are a man or a woman, crying will cause others to question your strength and competence. No, this stereotype is not fair or true, but it is powerful. The mocking stories that can result from a crying incident die hard. I was once in a meeting years after an attorney had left the firm and unwillingly heard the tale of her tears.

Tip No. 13

No Scolding.

Scolding adults is inappropriate and ineffective.

Adversaries, subordinates, and sometimes even bosses occasionally deserve a good scolding. Of course, you want your colleagues and those who support your work to perform at a high level. Scolding adults is inappropriate and ineffective.

Scolding is a technique that parents use with children. If scolding is the only technique in your toolbox for correcting bad performance or other misdeeds, research other techniques. Try to find a technique that is encouraging and positive, techniques that inquire about how the unacceptable outcome came to pass, that identify the reasons the outcome is not acceptable, and describe a list of preferred outcomes; and, at least one future process for arriving at an acceptable outcome.

Scolding shuts down exploration and conversation. Mistakes need to be explored and discussed so that meaningful and lasting corrective measures can be adopted.

Tip No. 14

No Blaming.

Blaming others is almost always a losing proposition. Blame creates strife and division. It is also disempowering. It makes you a victim of someone else's behaviors and choices. It ignores the behaviors and choices within your control that contributed to the undesirable outcome.

Instead of blaming, be accountable for your role in the situation and take responsibility for collaboratively creating a winning solution. Blaming invites people out. No one wants to be at fault, and no one wants to be part of a messy situation. Accountability and responsibility are model team-building behaviors. Notice the difference in the energy that says, "You broke this situation, now fix it!" and the energy that says, "Let us get together and find a solution to this challenge."

So much energy is wasted on blame and defense, and corporate cultures that encourage this approach often devolve into back-biting, cutthroat hierarchies.

Tip No. 15

No Petting.

Keep your hands to yourself is one rule from our childhood that we should apply in the corporate workplace. Other than the bland handshake, touching others is a red-zone behavior. I bet someone reading this is thinking, "Surely, a pat on the back, a handhold, or a shoulder massage is okay, right?" Wrong! While there are studies that show that we need touch, and that touch increases truthfulness and feelings of affinity, the risks of touching are great.

Even petting with the consent of the person being petted may make others who are not being petted feel uncomfortable. And, it may cause higher-ups in the company to take the wrong kind of notice.

Like the bottom-line of many of these tips, you want to be noticed for the right reasons; petting coworkers (or anyone else on the job) is not the right reason.

Tip No. 16

No Excessive Surfing.

Part of my job involved writing use policies for computers, the internet, and office equipment. These policies emphasized the fact that the individual had no right to privacy concerning anything done on or stored on or in office equipment. Employers may monitor the amount and content of internet use. So, use care and common sense in your surfing. Even if it appears that no one is watching, surf as if someone is!

Tip No. 17

No Elicit Emailing.

I am amazed at the type of information that can often be found on employee computers. Some contain incredibly embarrassing information that discusses extramarital affairs, swinging, even pornography. All sent, received, or stored on very non-private office computers. DO NOT DO IT, NOT EVEN ONCE!

Tip No. 18

Do Not Do Any Work, Send Any Emails, or Store Any Documents that Can Get You Fired If Discovered.

Here is another great one. Do not email criticism of your boss or sexist or racist comments about other employees. Do not receive or send jokes or inappropriate political propaganda that could get you fired if it lands in the wrong hands, because it may. Do not maintain a paper trail on the office computer if you are planning to sue your employer or divorce your spouse. Overall, do not take any action on your work computer that could get you fired if discovered.

Tip No. 19

Do Not Gossip.

There is an old saying that amounts to: He who gossips with you will gossip about you. Office gossip is inevitable. The goal is to avoid being its perpetuator or subject. And, do not initiate gossip. You do not want your byline on anything negative. Whether it is true or false, being the "he-said" or "she-said" associated with the tale makes you wrong.

In a world full of gossipers, a non-gossiper is invaluable. That person becomes the holder of secrets because that person is a safe space where others can place their trust.

Tip No. 20

Choose Carefully When Involving Yourself with Peers.

Friendships are beautiful. Yet, at work, you truly are known by the company you keep. Excessive involvement or cliquishness with peers can be off-putting or alienating to other colleagues. It is best to be inclusive and friendly, while honoring and maintaining professional boundaries. You never want to be in a position where friendship loyalties force you to choose sides in a political office battle.

Tip No. 21

Identify and Remain Loyal to a Mentor.

If you can develop a mentor/mentee relationship with one of your supervisors or another senior person, be excessively and publicly loyal to your mentor (without violating any of the other DOs and DON'Ts). Loyalty attracts the right kind of attention. The word will get around. Your mentor will be flattered and inspired to support you more and others will be favorably envious.

Tip No. 22

Protect Your Bosses and Be Publicly Loyal to Them.

Everything that applies to your mentor applies doubly to your boss. Sometimes, it is hard to be positive about a boss either because the boss does not deserve it or because it feels like brown-nosing. Even if you cannot be positive, remember there is no safe space to criticize your boss (with the possible exception of your own home, assuming you do not share a living space with someone from the office). Others may have the privilege to criticize the boss without punishment; do not assume that you do. Stay loyal and do not air your dirty laundry in public.

Tip No. 23

Criticism Often Backfires.

There is no safe place at the job for ridicule of anyone, including your significant other, the government, or a business competitor or vendor. Be known as the person who brings harmony to situations, not the one who brings friction. That does not mean you should not stand for what you believe in. Just be a stand in a substantive way without ridiculing anyone or anything.

Tip No. 24

Publicly Maintain a Positive Attitude.

Not obnoxiously. Not transparently. Just honestly speak what is good. Find the reasons the cup is half full. Do not join the hoard of whining complainers. If your complaints are insignificant, they may be off-putting to those with real challenges. If your complaints are significant, they may become fodder for negative rumors. If you have small complaints, self-soothe and know there are those suffering worse. If the complaints are real, remember that a negative attitude drains your creative energy, and remember that complaints are false action. Take real action. Be creative. And, cause the desired change.

Tip No. 25

Be Eager.

Eagerness is a more specific aspect of maintaining a positive attitude. Your eagerness will take you places and get you on projects others miss. Eagerness reminds more experienced and seasoned colleagues of their days of eagerness and excitement. It reignites and ignites energy in others. Eagerness makes a job that has to be done more fun to do and adds to the enjoyment of all who participate. Stay balanced. Do not bite off more than you can chew. Do not overdo it. Just allow yourself to experience eagerness about doing whatever you endeavor to do. Eagerness also will stir your internal fire, which will add to your ability to succeed!

Tip No. 26

Let It Be Widely Known that You Love What You Do.

This is a more specific aspect of maintaining a positive public attitude. When supervisors assign work, they do not want to feel bad about doing it. They want to give it to someone willing. A willing attitude will keep you working, especially if you work in a place where billable hours are tracked.

Tip No. 27

Be Confident,
But Not Overconfident.

Overconfidence and arrogance are different words for the same off-putting behavior. Do not be cocky. Just know what you ought to know, and do not second-guess yourself. True story. A boss once asked me how to spell a word. I said, "I think you spell it . . .." The boss then went to my colleague and asked how to spell the word. She said, "You spell it . . .." My colleague spelled it exactly as I did. The boss then went and looked it up. He saw our spelling was right. He next went and thanked my colleague and told her she was right. I went and asked, "Why didn't you thank me? I gave you the same spelling." His answer, "Because you said you were unsure!" Be sure. Know what you know and stand in what you know.

Tip No. 28

Be Truthful.

Tiny lies may seem insignificant, even beneficial. But, in the long run, absolute credibility is far more valuable than the challenges you evade by lying. This is most important with dealing with competitors or the opposition. Being known as a "straight shooter" will increase your negotiating leverage in every situation. You can create context around the truth but tell the truth.

Tip No. 29

Be Diplomatic.

This is a more specific aspect of maintaining a positive attitude and telling the truth. Negative situations need to be couched in a positive context. For example, this negative thing has these positive aspects, and I have a few suggestions on how we can respond to the negative aspects. People want problem-solvers, not problem-presenters!

Tip No. 30

Be Direct.

This may be a head-scratcher. You may be asking, how can I be diplomatic and direct at the same time, and how do I know when to be direct and when to be diplomatic? These all work together. This is part of telling the truth. You can tell the truth in a diplomatic, problem-solving fashion, but do not be so diplomatic that the truth is covered up or made to seem less significant than it is. Granted, this is an art. But it is an art that you can become incredibly good at with a little practice. Notice the successful people around you. Chances are they are employing this strategy. Model what they do or get some business coaching if you feel unsure.

Tip No. 31

Be Well-Liked by Opponents.

The number one mistake many people make on the job is to see their opponents as enemies. Your opponents also have many opportunities to weigh in on your performance and character. They play a significant role in determining your reputation. Someday, you may even find yourself looking to them for a job. The primary principle here: there are no disposable people. See the value of everyone you encounter.

Tip No. 32

Leave Your Personal Life at Home, Verbally, and Attitudinally.

Consider carefully before sharing personal information.

This is another critical part of rumor avoidance. Avoid discussing your personal life. Even if it is as impersonal as talking about in-laws or vacation, it can become fodder for others to discuss outside of your presence. For example, if your in-laws are wealthy, the rumor may begin that your spouse has money. People may become curious as to how your household finances are handled, and, curious as to whether the in-laws helped to buy the house. If you discuss your vacation, it may raise questions. Where did you go? How long were you gone? How did you afford it? Should you be spending more time at work?

Many people are bored on the job, and your life provides a nice diversion. The gossiping may not be malicious, but it may land in the ear of someone with bad intentions. Remember, nothing is benign. Consider carefully before sharing personal information.

Also, leave your personal life at home attitudinally. Your bad personal life can easily become your bad professional life if you are not conscientious. Notwithstanding breakups, child-rearing issues, even parental illness, your attitude, and focus at work needs to be consistent. People will forgive you for slip-ups in this area, but unfortunately, they will also remember you as unreliable in a clench, inconsistent, and unable to handle the pressure. You are a human being. You may not always be able to do what I am suggesting, but just do not make emotional breakdowns a part of your work routine.

Tip No. 33

Acknowledge Personal Crises that Directly Impact Your Work Performance.

When a crisis rises to the level that it interferes with your work performance, it is time to bring in some support. First, develop a plan for responding to the crisis. Make sure it is realistic. Build in wiggle room, because plans are just plans and things do not always go as planned. When you have your external support and plan, identify a trusted insider, and share your situation and your plan. Your goal is to receive guidance and have someone in power who is armed with information and well-positioned to advocate for you if necessary.

Tip No. 34

No Sexism. No Racism. No Homophobia.

These three should be obvious. If they are not, figure out how to resolve your issues and not air them at work. Tip: being in an oppressed group does not give you a free pass to oppress others or to make offensive statements. Also, watch yourself. If you feel uncomfortable with people for one of these three reasons or another reason, it could cause you to short-circuit your communications and sabotage your working relationship and your performance.

Tip No. 35

Do Not Deride or Defend Peers.

Sometimes when you like or dislike a peer, or when you hear something being said that is inaccurate or unfair, you will want to get involved. You may want to pile on when someone you dislike is being attacked. Or you may want to defend when someone you like is attacked unfairly. (I confess I was a defender of others.) Avoid either course of action. Appear compassionate to incompetence.

Tip No. 36

Do Not Cut Corners.

Time pressure and workload demands may tempt you to take shortcuts. Do not do it! Shortcuts too often lead to big problems. They are short-term fixes with long-term regrets. This is especially true in cases where the work you do has a long lifecycle. Shortcutting something important can result in a haunting fear that lasts much longer than it would have taken to simply do the work properly in the first place. If you are stuck in a situation that demands corner-cutting, it probably means your time management or workload management needs addressing. Look at the bigger picture and fix the real problem.

Tip No. 37

Business Casual Does Not Mean Business Bum.

Without being flashy, dress at the level that is expected, not at the level you think you can get away with. This is another thing that people take note of without saying anything to you. If you do not hear any negative feedback, it does not necessarily mean people have not taken negative notice. Similarly, do not overdress or be too flashy. The point of your attire is professionalism. No matter what level of attire is expected, keep your clothing clean, neat, and nice but not overly memorable.

Tip No. 38

Do Not Date or Sleep with Anyone Employed by the Company.

Again, this may seem obvious, but many employees believe that if the person they have relations with is not a subordinate, then the relationship is okay. The fallout of a bad relationship among peers, while different than that of a relationship where sexual harassment is an issue, can still be catastrophic and at a minimum distracting. Dating those you work with is lazy dating. There are so many folks outside the job to choose from. Choose one of them.

Tip No. 39

Get Involved.

Without forfeiting your identity or compromising your work ethic, participate in non-work-related activities hosted by your job, its clients, vendors, or the industry. Find the events that authentically interest you. Sports teams, happy hours, fundraisers, volunteering in a soup kitchen—you decide. Just make it something you will enjoy. Experiencing joy with the people at your job, in a non-work-related way, strengthens relationships and allows you to view others and be viewed by others from a new and warmer vantage point. But here is a tip. There really is no non-work-related setting. If people from your job are present, job dynamics are present. Do not get so relaxed that you forget that.

Tip No. 40

Be Polite.

This does not mean being a pushover or not enforcing boundaries. It simply means that on-the-job and in life, courtesy goes a long way. It has no real downside, and it demonstrates respect for the people with whom you come in contact. So, as Nike says: Just do it!

Tip No. 41

Watch Your Body Language.

A closed angry body, a depressed sullen body, or an exhausted unhappy body disinvites the success you desire. Keep your body language positive. Be upright, energized, and open. And, remember, the best way to keep your body language positive is to keep your mind positive. Your body tells the truth about how you feel; so, do your work and identify a process for aligning your feelings and infusing your body with life.

Tip No. 42

Pay Attention to Advice.

Many times, big messages, messages from on high, messages that can mean the difference between success and failure, are conveyed subtly and softly. Do not dismiss advice because it is presented as "not a big deal" or because it is offered by a person who is low on the totem pole. Often, important messages are delivered through a whisper campaign and become either amplified or diluted with each new messenger. Identify the value in the message and take it to heart. It may just save your job!

Tip No. 43

Create New Work for Yourself.

Suggest projects, clients, research, new areas to explore. Do what it takes to stay busy. I am not talking about churning time unnecessarily. I am talking about inventing new opportunities for yourself and the job. This adds to your perceived value and to the value you gain from the job.

Tip No. 44

Request Training.

On self-identified or management-identified weaknesses, request training. If you realize or are told that you need to improve in an area, do something about it. If you think you have the power to fix the issue on your own, try it, but check in to ensure that you have improved. Weaknesses that are genuine weaknesses (not just those that are the result of a lack of sleep or a tough emotional period), do not just go away on their own. There is no shame in getting support.

There is no shame in getting support.

Getting support says that you value your job and yourself! It says you are willing to take the initiative to better your performance. Even if you do not improve, your efforts to become better will be recognized and appreciated. You may even find that you are valuable enough that your position can be massaged so you no longer have to do the thing you are not good at doing.

Tip No. 45

Use Care When Involving Yourself in Pro-Bono or Charitable Projects.

No matter what is said publicly, unpaid work (charitable, pro bono, and/or nonbillable work) usually carries less weight than paid work (billable). In choosing the type, and extent of unpaid work you will do, remember unpaid work can support you in gaining skills and visibility. It can be a win-win. Just do not lose sight of the fact that you have a few short years to make your value known, to learn transferable skills, to make your company (or firm) believe that they are better off with you than without you. No matter how good unpaid work makes you feel, balance this work, and make sure it does not amount to the lion's share of your time.

Tip No. 46

Do Not Get a Reputation for Socializing.

Socialize enough, but not too much. Do not show up first or leave last. This is another one of the ways that you want to be unremarkable. Be a strong networker, be charismatic, be charming, but be balanced.

Tip No. 47

Evaluate Subordinates Honestly.

Do not puff up or tear down subordinates falsely. Say what is true. Your falseness serves no one. Your subordinates get better with honest feedback.

Tip No. 48

Get Clients.

If you have clients, your faults are more forgivable. Clients are clout. If your clients are committed to you, they give you leverage at your present employer and make you attractive to new employers. But, most importantly, they empower you with confidence and illustrate your future potential. If you do not work at a job where employees cultivate individual clients, cultivate people who ask for you by name. Cultivate people who notice if you are off work or on vacation. Having people favorably notice you, conveys a message to your employer that you are noteworthy.

Tip No. 49

Know Trends in the Area of Your Specialization and News and Current Events, But Do Not Be Overly Opinionated.

The facts that you know are valuable, and knowing those facts increases your value, especially if you develop a reputation for having such knowledge. Your opinion is great if someone has requested it. If no one has requested it, adding your opinion may be unwanted, and it may make you seem like a know-it-all or a blowhard. A reputation as either of these is harmful and nullifies the positive benefits of knowing the information in the first place. If people know they will have to endure your unwanted opinions, they will be less likely to use you as an informational resource, thus decreasing your value.

Tip No. 50

Have a Sense of Humor!

Laughter is stress-relieving. It helps you and the people around you to relax. Being able to laugh authentically, especially at yourself, evidences a level of maturity and naturally increases trust. So, drop the formality, break the tension, and invite a sense of common humanity by having a sense of humor.

Tip No. 51

Exhibit Your Best Personality, Not Your Worst.

Most of us are capable of being an ass and an angel. People tolerate and sometimes fear an ass. Mistakenly, some believe that fear is a good thing. But, I think you will agree that being tolerated and feared does not feel as good as being respected, trusted, and admired. Those who are tolerated and feared often do not get the extra effort or the extra intel that people give to co-workers they like. This extra effort and extra intel can mean the difference between success and failure. So, keep the ass-ism to a minimum.

Tip No. 52

Come to the Table with a Plan or Suggestion.

Do not just announce problems and obstacles. Even if your suggestions are not adopted, the fact that you thought beyond the problem will be noticed. Your failed idea may inspire a better, more effective idea. Remember how many useless filaments were tried in the lightbulb before an effective one was identified.

Tip No. 53

Follow Through.

All of us have a sense of the sacred nature of a promise.

Once upon a time the slang phrase "word is bond" was popular. In other times and other parts of this society, a man's word was considered as good as a contract. All of us have a sense of the sacred nature of a promise.

We have an ancient subconscious predisposition that causes us to value those who do what they say they will do. Whether it is as small as calling at the time arranged, or as large as making a million-dollar payment, whatever it is you say you will do, do it! If you absolutely cannot do it, do not try to worm your way out of it. Stand up, acknowledge your promise, state your inability to follow through, and request to negotiate a new arrangement that honors the needs of the other person and your own needs. Then, follow through on that!

Tip No. 54

Beware: Publicly Challenging a Colleague, Co-Worker or Boss Is an Invitation to Open Conflict.

Instead, hold private discussions and raise opposing views as "other possibilities." If it is a point you need to win, make sure you raise it at the right time with the right person. Another approach is to have it raised by a surrogate with more power or authority and who is more likely to be heard and listened to with deference.

Tip No. 55

Do Not Pilfer Supplies.

This may seem obvious. It should be. Again, go back to grade school. If it does not belong to you, do not take it. This is where thinking you and your job are a "we" (identity-melding) can and does create problems. When you see yourself and your job as one, then what is theirs becomes yours. Boundaries become enmeshed. You are not your job. Their supplies do not belong to you and should not be used for personal purposes. It could seriously damage your reputation and future.

Tip No. 56

Know that What You Say Will Travel.

Even the best jobs are like small-town rumor mills. Do not expect your words to remain secret. What you say in private will come to light, so apply this well-known test. Ask yourself, is it true? Is it kind? Is it necessary?[23] If "no" is the answer to any of these questions, reconsider. Instead of sharing what you have to say on the job, you have the power to make a different choice.

Tip No. 57

Purchase a Home, a Car, or Whatever Else Makes Sense for You. But, Do Not Overextend.

Homeownership says stability. Overextending is tantamount to signing up for slavery. Save, pay off debt, and work towards financial freedom. This is the royal lifestyle, the freedom to stay at your job, or leave if you please. Give yourself room and the freedom to grow into the person you are to become, instead of being imprisoned by a paycheck.

Tip No. 58

Do Not Hide, Tell Them Who You Are.

I experience ADD and I am Black, female, same-sex loving, and proud. Because of the many "isms" that are practiced in the world, on the job many hide aspects of themselves. This hiding creates a subtle tension. Withholding creates an energy of mistrust. In contrast, authenticity builds trust. Telling the truth about who you are is authentic, positions you to be protected by laws that prohibit illegal discrimination.

Tip No. 59

Expect to Bear the Burden of Miscommunications.

Oftentimes, people cope with work issues by intentionally being ambiguous, pretending not to have understood the assignment, pretending not to have understood what was agreed to in the telephone conversation or pretending not to have understood expectations. While it may feel comfortable, it is not a viable strategy. Even when people legitimately fail to understand and act from a place of misunderstanding, they are judged negatively for failing to ask questions and failing to gain clarity. Be clear, and if you are not clear, get clear, do not fake it!

Tip No. 60

To Gain New Recruits or Clients Your Firm or Company May Attempt to Use Your Status as a Minority or Any Other Status You Hold.

At the highest levels, individuals exploit their family, friendships, religious groups, political spheres, and whatever other networks they have access to so that they can achieve their goals.

While you may not want to become the spokesmodel for your group, know that this type of use is common across all lines of difference and similarity. It may feel like you are being singled out, and you may not like it; but, remember that your company will always attempt to draw from you all the value you have, including any value that comes from your identity. At the highest levels, individuals exploit their family, friendships, religious groups, political spheres, and whatever other networks they have access to so that they can achieve their goals.

They will expect the same of you. Success at accomplishing the result of winning new clients or recruits is your job's goal. Your job will expect that to be your goal. If you can win recruits or clients without exploiting your networks that is great. If not, and you still refuse to exploit those networks, you may be judged as less valuable. The same is true if you attempt to exploit your networks and fail, (unless you demonstrate balancing value in some other area).

Tip No. 61

Check-in.

Do not travel too far down a path on a project without checking-in with the person who assigned it. When accepting an assignment tell the assigning person your planned approach and get their feedback. Ask good and necessary questions. Do not pretend to understand what is being asked of you if you do not. When you believe you are clear, send an e-mail confirming your understanding of their guidance and laying out how you will proceed.

Tip No. 62

Do Not Get Lost.

Do not get lost in your pet aspect of an assignment, no matter how interesting it may seem. Do what has been asked of you first. Then, if there is additional time, you may explore your pet interest in the topic. If you allow your interests to overshadow what you have been asked to do, you are taking a big risk. If you are right and your angle is the angle, all may be okay, or the assignor may be resentful. The assignor may feel like you were insubordinate, ignored instructions, and attempted to upstage them. If your angle is not the angle, the assignor may feel like you wasted time, displayed arrogance, ignored instructions, and attempted to be the smartest guy or girl in the room. If you do what you were instructed to do and then follow your interest as an extra effort, you will convey reliability, industry, and initiative. And, any negative feelings the assignor may have about what you have done will be offset a bit by the fact that you did what you were asked to do first.

Tip No. 63

Delegate, as Necessary.

Yes, when appropriate, delegate. But never entrust someone with a task that is so important you could be fired if it is done wrong. For example, I once had a statutory deadline for the filing of a client's request for an appeal of an administrative decision. In short, it was a deadline that could not be extended. My document needed to be submitted by the end of the business day on the day that I completed it. Because of a series of mishaps, I was right up against the wire and had about 30 minutes to get my document where it had to be. Though we had reserved a courier to run it over, in the end, I decided to go myself. Some may argue that it was a waste of my time. But here is what happened: street closings and traffic made a twenty-minute drive take 35 minutes. When I arrived, the office was closed. I got myself in the building, got myself to the office, spoke desperately through the door to a remaining staff person, got instructions on how to get it delivered and stamped after hours, and knew from then on how to file documents up until 11:59 pm! This information added to my value and saved my job. The firm's courier had no idea this was possible. Given all I did to get through traffic, get in the building, get to the right office, get the information on the after-hours filing, and get the document filed, there is no doubt in my mind that the courier would not have succeeded in getting my document filed. And, I would have suffered the consequences! The other lesson here is do not ever let 30 minutes stand between you and the loss of your job. Meet your deadlines with a healthy buffer to spare!

Tip No. 64

Get Familiar.

Before you need to use it, become familiar with the use of equipment, research tools, or whatever else may be needed to do your job. It is much less stressful to learn how to use what you need when there is no urgency attached.

Tip No. 65

Make Friends with Support People.

Hint: Everyone is a support person! Librarians and copy center employees, people in billing, people in accounting, people in legal all are support people. The more people in various departments that you know and love, the more success you will have. People can grease the wheels for you. No matter how smart or competent you are, everybody needs a wheel greased occasionally. Also, different departments receive information at different times, knowing people in other departments expands the scope of information to which you will have access.

Tip No. 66

Be Independent.

Today, if your job requires the use of the computer, you are expected to be able to accomplish what needs to be done on your own. You will be competing with people who know how to do exactly that. If you cannot, you are at a disadvantage.

You do not want your work to suffer because of someone else.

If you have one, treat your secretary well and treat him or her and all other support staff as a luxury. Over a ten-year career in a law firm, I had at least five secretaries that I can remember; three, who were excellent. And, that was good; but, soon after their excellence became known (I foolishly bragged about them), they were offered opportunities and advanced. Regardless of loyalty, most people will accept opportunities to advance (and it is only fair that they should). Also, if you advance or change departments, your secretary or assistants may stay behind. As you advance, your workload may be too much for your assistant to maintain if he or she is a shared assistant. If that is the case and you are low man or woman in the ranks, expect your work to be low on the assistant's priority list. The bottom line is that you do not want your work to suffer because of someone else.

You should know where your files are, how to access everything related to what you do or have done, and how to get things done on your own. Finally, while it is wonderful to have friends and to be friendly with those who assist you, do not overshare. I had a partner that checked in with my secretary on how I was doing. He would ask if my timesheets were done, had I begun work on a brief that was due—that kind of thing. Fortunately, my secretary was an ally and let me know when he did this (maybe he expected her to, I do not know), and I would then have an idea of what he was concerned about; but, things could have gone very differently. Assistants talk, secretaries talk, so the rule with them is the same as with everyone else: do not confide what you do not want to be shared with others. Your secrets are yours to keep. Do not share the burden of your secrets with others, especially those who others above you in the food chain may compel to answer questions about you.

Tip No. 67

Have Facetime!

Be seen at the job. Facetime was a thing long before Apple added it as a feature on the iPhone. It is important to *presence* yourself at the job. No matter how compelling the reason, frequent absences hurt you, and disappearing hurts you. People are always noticing the behavior of those they work with, and even if you think you are being clever, someone knows; and, where one knows, all know. Play it straight! While people may not blame you for being absent if your reasons are valid; regardless of the validity of your reasons, they will consciously or unconsciously choose to rely on the people consistently available. Make yourself one of those people! When you must be away from your job, *presence* yourself at the job using text, email, and phone. Make sure people know that you are accessible. If you are out with clients or at hearings, subtly make sure they know that too!

Tip No. 68

Have Enough Work to Be Able to Come in on the Weekend.

You may not choose to work every weekend, but for workflow purposes, you should ensure that you have enough work cued up to work the weekend. If not, you are probably underutilized, which you never want to be. Plan! Ask for or generate new work, before all your work is complete. Here is an example of how to generate work: "Joe, remember that project I did for you on Smith Mining? I read in the *Wall Street Journal* the other day that their competitor Avery Mining was just charged with twelve violations. Do you think Smith would like us to look into that and drop them a memo on the details and ways to avoid being charged with similar violations?" Whether this approach works or not, you have shown Joe that you are keeping current on issues of concern to clients, that you are hungry for advancement, and that you enjoy working with him, because you brought the work to him. A question like this increases your value. If you think you are too busy, you probably have not learned to juggle. You want to ensure that you have work in the queue that has varying deadlines and levels of importance. Though you cannot always avoid it, you do not want too many critical projects due at the same time.

Generating the kind of work that I outlined above is a good way to put a few low-level projects in your pocket to work on when you need hours and to push to the side when you need to focus on critical deadline-driven projects. Finally, work a few of those weekends, ideally in the office, but from home if necessary. You want to be busy in fact and appear busy on paper. Your billable time, your known workload, and your facetime should pretty much align.

Tip No. 69

Do Not Be Intimidated by Bosses.

Being intimidated by your bosses is like a football player being afraid to be tackled. Be respectful, be cautious; but, be a stand for yourself. Go get what it takes for you to succeed, get the mentoring, the advice, and all the takeaways you can gather through their example.

Tip No. 70

Do Not Be Intimidated by the Ambition of Others.

Most jobs are tortoise and hare situations. Meaning your success occurs through the long arch of time. The overly ambitious often burn out, step on the wrong toes, intimidate those above them and suffer because of it, or simply seize other opportunities. Do not worry about others. Play your own game and be excellent at it. If you do, your value will keep you on the job for as long as you desire to be there.

Tip No. 71

Be Thoughtful.

When you go to grab food, occasionally ask your secretary or the building security guard if they want you to bring something back. Remember to ask about children and ailing parents. Remember hobbies and pet peeves. I had a boss who loved baseball memorabilia, so for his son's bar mitzvah, I gave him a valuable baseball card. I hope the son liked it, but I know the dad liked it. Note, this was not a manipulation! I liked this boss, and I believed he would love for his son to own this card. Being thoughtful is not brownnosing. It also is not the same as oversharing your personal information. It is a way of demonstrating to others that you "see" them. It is reminding yourself and those you work with that we are all human beings, and all have a value that extends far beyond the work we do at the job.

Tip No. 72

Do Not Be Silent.

When something needs to be said, be tactful and diplomatic if necessary, but say it. If you allow mistakes to occur or information to be overlooked because you were too timid to speak, things will not go well for you. If it is discovered that you knew or were positioned to know something vital that you did not say, you will be blamed. You do not have to be a blabbermouth, and you should not be a gossip; but, be present, and presence yourself in the room by participating. Do not be invisible, do not wait to be called out or invited into the conversation. Offer, volunteer, not obnoxiously or overbearingly; but, enough to be viewed as involved, and enough to stir the fires of contribution in your soul.

Tip No. 73

Confront But Do Not Be Confrontational.

Now and then, you will need to confront someone at work about something. Do it with a smile! I was once in a hiring committee meeting where a person, far more senior than I, railed on minority hiring fairs claiming that we never got any good people from these job fairs and that they were a waste of our time and money. This was in a room of fewer than ten people, all partners except me (that is another long story), in which I was the sole Black person, and maybe the only woman (I cannot remember). Also, I had come to work for the firm via one of these hiring fairs. So, all eyes turned to me, though I do not think he meant his statement to be an attack on me. Privilege may have blinded him such that he did not notice I was in the room or consider how I arrived there. What did I do? I waited for him to finish and after his foot was firmly lodged in his mouth, I cleared my throat, took a

Humor and subtlety can make the point and, importantly, allow the other person to save face and exit the situation gracefully.

sip of water, smiled, and said: "Well, Joe (which is an arbitrary name I am choosing to apply in this book to all the males I reference), does that mean I am not a good one? I was hired through one of those job fairs." And, I kept smiling and waiting for him to answer. He turned redder and redder and kept shaking his head like my Blackness was something that had escaped him up until that moment, then he sputtered something like, "No, no, I didn't mean you, I didn't, I didn't know, didn't remember. Really? Really? You were hired through one of those? Well, I guess I stand corrected then, I guess sometimes they do . . .." And, his voice petered away to nothing, at which point the person in charge of the meeting said: "Well, I guess that is answered then; let's move on." And we did! The point is that you do not have to become a barking dog to confront someone. Humor and subtlety can make the point and, importantly, allow the other person to save face and exit the situation gracefully.

How you handle confrontation will determine whether those you confront become friends and allies or enemies and opponents.

Tip No. 74

Do Keep Options Open But Do Not Be Indiscreet in Seeking Other Employment.

Your clients and vendors, competitors, and opponents are also potential future employers and colleagues. Be sure to treat them as such. Show them your best side and keep the sniping to a minimum. Most jobs focus on a specific industry and within these industries, the players rotate but often remain the same. Being known as likable, excellent, and professional will carry you a long way. If you are a member of a minority group, keeping a tight network is even more important. Yet, remember that discretion is the better part of valor. No one wants to be dumped, and if your current employer learns that you are actively fielding other offers, it may not go well for you. I know of a woman who was fired because one of her bosses saw the woman's resume on the competitor's desk while at a meeting. No one ever knew if the competitor had put the resume on the desk on purpose, or even maliciously told the boss about his disloyal employee; but in the end, it did not matter. She got one of those "it has come to our attention that you are not happy here" meetings and soon, sooner than she was prepared for, she was out the door.

Tip No. 75

Pick a Mentor in the Middle, Not Too Big or Too Small a Fish.

Do not settle for a mentor you are given, though you should value and attempt to bond with that person. Pick someone you would like to emulate, and someone you believe would be willing to aid you in succeeding. Big fish are busy, too far removed from where you are in the pecking order, and are unlikely to remember how hard it was to be where you are or exactly how they succeeded in making it through. A small fish is still in the throes of their own survival experience and may not be willing to give you the keys to what they are still trying to make THEIR kingdom. A middle fish is focused on the next rung of the ladder and is less likely to be threatened by your desire to advance. The middle fish may even be flattered that you have chosen him over a big fish. After all, by choosing him you are saying, "I see you as a success!"

Tip No. 76

Ask Open-Ended Questions.

This is great guidance for on the job and in life. Of course, make sure you have time to listen to the answers. Open-ended questions allow a person to provide a full answer that involves variables and context and disclaimers, and all that you need to know that you would not have found out if you had just asked a yes-or-no question. For example, "Is there a bathroom nearby?" might get you an answer like, "Yes, down the hall to the left." Whereas, an open-ended question like, "What's the bathroom situation like here?" may get you an answer like this, "Well, the one down the hall to the left is the biggest, but it is also the busiest and the dirtiest. I like the one down the hall to the right; it is a one-staller and private if you know what I mean!" The second answer provides additional valuable information that the yes-or-no answer left out. In the second answer, the person responding is confiding in you. You are now their secret bathroom buddy. Open-ended questions not only yield more information, but they also increase intimacy and open the door to better relationships.

Tip No. 77

Ask *"How Did You?"* Questions. *"If You Were Me, How Would You?"* Questions. *"What Would You Suggest?"* Questions.

All these questions take the answerer back to their own experience and allow them to talk about most people's favorite subject, themselves. Even the, "If you were me?" question causes them to put themselves in your shoes, to think about how they are the same or different than you, and to feel a certain level of commonality with you. In short, it inspires them to want to assist you. On the other hand, if you ask a "What should I do?" question, you are shifting responsibility for yourself over to them. No one wants to take responsibility for you on the job. No one wants to be the one you point to when someone asks why you made the mistake you made. It is for you to know what you should do, not someone else. Unless the "someone else" is your boss of course, then it is perfectly acceptable to ask, "How do you want this handled?" or, "How should we handle this?" or even "How should I handle this?" It is your boss's job to be the one that stands between you and the potential mistakes you would make if you had not consulted him. Still, even with your boss, it is good to come armed with your ideas for resolution, so that he knows you are capable of figuring things out alone if need be. Your ideas let the boss see how your judgment is developing and how he or she can support you in tweaking it if necessary.

Tip No. 78

Be Switzerland. Stay Neutral.

At every job, there are power struggles. Try not to get caught in the middle of them. Though I admit, this is easier said than done. You sometimes may be the object of the struggle. If you have multiple bosses or multiple people assigning work to you, they may silently or subtly begin to compete over who commands your time and attention. This battle is dangerous for you! Be on the lookout for it, and when it shows up, stay neutral and attempt to neutralize it. You can neutralize it by not fueling it. Let the two battle it out without you engaging in frustration or stress over their competing deadlines or directives. Neutrally, not frantically, inform them of competing time demands and then direct them to one another for resolution. For example, "Joe, I'd love to do that for you. I really would. Josephine has me doing something right now that is time sensitive. Would you be willing to work it out with her to see if it is okay for me to tackle both assignments?" Do not let crazy people or crazy situations make you crazy. Immunize yourself against the crazy contagion by practicing transparency and good communications.

Tip No. 79

Do Not Be Baited.

Keep your personal political views personal.

Unless it is a political firm and you share its politics, stay low-key on politics and political issues. Many jobs spread political money and support across the spectrum to people who have the power to influence the industry the company is involved in. They may support a candidate, not for his or her overall position on issues, or status as a conservative or progressive; they may support the candidate to have the candidate's ear on the issue or issues important to them. For this reason, they may even fund candidates who oppose each other. This funding happens in all kinds of interesting ways that are not relevant to our discussion. What is relevant is that it is not about personal views on issues; it is about how the candidate can help or hurt the business or the industry. Keep your personal political views personal.

Fund the candidates and issues that you want to fund. On a personal level follow your heart. Do not be baited into conversations or confrontations with others, even colleagues on these issues. If you allow yourself to be baited, news of your position and (especially if you are a minority) of your passionate or angry outburst will spread. You do not want to be known as an angry outburst person.

Tip No. 80

Do Not Be Obvious in Circumventing the Chain of Command or Whistleblowing.

I do not believe in whistleblowing over minor issues, and I think there is often much more to lose by jumping the chain of command than by following it. However, there are those times when whistleblowing cannot be helped. When someone is attempting to engage you in something that is unethical or illegal or is harassing you in ways that are illegal or inappropriate, you have a right to act. The problem is that even in these situations where your action is more than warranted, the job may not appreciate it. In this case, when I say the job, I mean those in power at the job who hold your future in their hands. This, again, is a time for subtlety. Do not take an overt action, such as filing a report with HR or having a closed-door meeting with higher management; not in the beginning. Instead, document, document, document, not on your work computer, but in a private space. Note what is happening and wait until you are positive and have documented definitive proof of what is happening. Then, find alternative causes to be in the company of those who need to know. In the course of conducting the other business, drop hints about what is happening. This may take more than one meeting; work slowly and make them pull it out of you. You do not want to be viewed as a willing provider of this damning news. Companies do not like whistleblowers. They just do not! You will be branded and distrusted until your career rots and you may even find it difficult to find other jobs. So, discretion with this is mandatory. And the answer to the question: "Who else have you told?" always should be, "No one, and please do not tell anyone else!" If you find yourself in a real tough situation like that, reach out to someone external who can offer you proper advice in context about how to move forward.

Tip No. 81

Do Show Interest and Volunteer for Work on Issues that Interest You.

Enthusiasm is irresistible and contagious. Show your job that you have it. The way to develop the responsibilities you enjoy is to design your job description; not the technical written description, but the daily lived experience of what you do on the job. Fill it with the things you enjoy by volunteering for those things and letting them fill your plate.

Tip No. 82

Keep Your Boss Informed.

When your boss is caught off-guard and you possess the missing information, your boss likely will blame you. If you know something you think your boss needs to know, tell her, or be prepared to permanently keep quiet. If it is about a fellow employee and you were told in confidence, then stay quiet. If it is a work development and you are assuming your boss knows or should know, make sure your boss does know. If it is something about you—vacations, pregnancy, marriage—do not make your boss wait to learn about it through the grapevine. If it is a scheduling issue, announce your intention in terms of the schedule, ask your boss to notify you if he or she has a challenge with your plan, and then send a reminder close to the date.

Bosses get busy and do not always do the work they need to do to be prepared for what is expected of them. This is where you come in. Remind them. Inform them. And, cover for them. This adds to your value and makes them want to keep you around. Letting them flounder in embarrassment, (instead of saving them) may seem tempting, but it will hurt you in the long run and put them in a bad mood that you will have to endure.

Tip No. 83

Spend Quality Time with Family.

Once lost, family time is time you cannot get back. Your kids are only going to grow up one time. You never want to hear your spouse say, "All you care about is work! I'm leaving because you work too much." You never want to have to weigh whether that statement is true or false. So, do not put yourself or your family in that position. Keep your priorities aligned and give your family the attention it needs to thrive. Yes, work weekends. But be careful not to work EVERY weekend. And, when you are sacrificing to be on the job, remember it is a sacrifice. Do not let yourself fall so in love with work that you routinely neglect your family without even noticing it. NOTICE IT! Be conscious of the sacrifice you are making, and without overworking the subject, let your job know that you value your family, despite your willingness to occasionally prioritize the job.

Tip No. 84

Check How You Are Progressing.

Come right out and ask the questions. "How am I doing? Am I progressing the way the company wants me to? What could I do better?" If there is a problem with your performance or otherwise, someone may volunteer information

Make it known that you are in it for the long haul and that you desire to perform and improve accordingly.

about the problem without you having to ask for it. But, they also may simply simmer in frustration about the problem, move on, spread the word to others, and penalize you by reducing the amount of work they send your way. You cannot take chances. Do not rely on or wait for your official evaluation. Ask! And while you are at it, let it be known that your goal is success and upward mobility. Some people come to a company or firm planning to stay only a few years, make a lot of money, and leave. These folks do not care how they are doing. They just hope to fly under the radar long enough to make their money and go. If you plan to stay and want to be promoted, you need to distinguish yourself from these people. Make it known that you are in it for the long haul and that you desire to perform and improve accordingly.

At the same time, most people do not work at the same job forever. Most do not ascend to senior executive status or partnership. So, keep that in mind and do not get too comfortable or too cozy. If necessary, advisable, or beneficial, leave. Today, companies value employees who have moved around more than employees who have stayed. Your chances for success increase when you change employers, rather than attempting to rise through the ranks, so be loyal to your career and then, if it makes sense, to your employer.

Tip No. 85

Stand for Yourself from the Very Beginning!

If you fail to be a stand for yourself at the outset, those who matter will assume that you will never stand for yourself. They will behave from that assumption. They will plan for you not to stand for yourself. When or if you finally do attempt to stand for yourself, your actions will upend their applecart. Then, your behavior, your effort to be a stand for yourself, will be met with resistance and resentment. By that point, you may never be allowed to stand for yourself within the company.

Tip No. 86

Negotiate Outcomes that You Desire.

There is no need to expend your capital fighting battles that you can address in a better way. Negotiation is a better way!

Do not just accept what is offered. This is a way that you can be a stand for yourself. On the job, things will be done to you and things will be taken from you. This is going to happen. You will not always have enough power to stop it. In many cases, wisdom will dictate that you avoid exhausting the power you have. In some cases, you will realize in advance that even though you may have the power to stop what is happening using that power would be unwise. The point is that there is no need to expend your capital fighting battles that you can address in a better way. Negotiation is a better way!

When you are faced with something you cannot change, let your disappointment with the situation be known. Then, do one of three things. Be a good sport and accept a chit, the promise of future consideration. (This is a risky strategy because chits lose their value over time, as memories fade.) Second, you could use the disappointing situation as leverage to get the company to grant you something unrelated that you want. Or third, you can use the disappointing situation to manage how the disappointing situation plays out; meaning that while you may not be able to stop it, you may be able to neutralize some of its objectionable aspects. Get creative! Creativity is a key negotiating skill.

Tip No. 87

Do Not Brown-nose.

No one likes brown-nosers, even those being kissed-up to. It will not yield the results you want. It is a poor substitute for good work. In most situations, it will not pay off, and it will cost you in terms of camaraderie with your peers. Brown-nosers are distrusted. Again, no one will tell you they distrust you. They will simply not share information with you and not include you in the circle of trust.

Tip No. 88

Do Not Step on Toes or Put Down Ideas.

Do not make anyone feel trampled upon.

If you are a volleyball player, you know how good a spike can feel. But, this is where I tell you to leave it on the court. No matter how easy the set-up or how vulnerable the other person is, do not seize the opportunity to crush them or their ideas. Even if it is the biggest jackass at the company or someone who has made you feel small in the past, do not go for the jugular. People never forget how you make them feel. So, do not make anyone feel trampled upon.

Use this method instead. Be heard, be firm, but tread lightly, ignore a bad idea by just acknowledging it, and moving forward, redirecting the conversation with alternative suggestions. If they force the issue, and they are so far afield as to be preposterous, have no fear, someone else will call it out. If there is no one else around, suggest that "we get another set of eyes on this." The same rule applies if the person with the slam-worthy idea is not there to hear the slam. This is the simple rule of doing unto others as you would want them to do unto you. People will remember your graciousness in not slamming others, and you will earn trust, respect, and known and unknown alliances.

Tip No. 89

Answer Questions to the Third Tier.

Oftentimes, when interacting with colleagues and bosses on the job, you can anticipate their reactions and questions. If you know the people you work with well and know your subject matter, it is easy to get good at this. What leaves a lot of people tongue-tied is that they do not prepare for the questions after the questions. We have all been in a room and watched someone deteriorate from ace to oaf. The stuttering and stammering begin, the "uhs" and "hmms;" and, then the uncomfortable silence engulfs the room. The person is stumped and embarrassed because they have been caught out there. They have been asked a question they have no answer for, and they have failed to tap dance around that obvious fact enough to get by. Anticipate questions you have no answer for. I am about to save you from ever being that person. Here is what you need to know. It is your boss's job to stump you.

If he cannot stump you, you have no business reporting to him. He has more expertise than you do. So, even though he may seem mortally wounded by your incompetence, he is secretly giving himself an "atta boy" for tripping you up. That said, be well prepared! Know the question that will come after the question you have been asked, and the question that will come after that. For example, let us say your boss has asked you to set up a meeting with the account representative at a vendor to discuss terms for a contract set to renew soon. You discover the account representative is away on vacation. Of course, you know your boss will want to know when the account representative will be back, so you are ready with that date. Great! And you also need to be able to remind the boss of the contract renewal date, tell the boss who is standing in for the account representative while he is on vacation, and what that person's availability is for a meeting. Finally, for extra points, you can tell the boss whether the vendor can negotiate a temporary extension so that your boss can meet with the regular representative if he chooses. Now, let's assume you have done all that and still your boss (possibly annoyed by your excellence) asks a question you cannot answer, such as where is the account representative vacationing, and can the account representative Skype while on vacation? This is when, instead of stammering, stuttering, or silence, you give the boss what he is looking for: affirmation that he is still the smartest guy in the room! You pause briefly, smile, and say that is a great idea, I will go check. Nine times out of ten, your boss will stop you from checking and direct you to pursue one of the avenues you had thought of already, but he just needed to let you know you had not thought of everything. He needed to affirm his value in the process, and by genuflecting, you allowed him to do so.

Tip No. 90

Specify the Parameters of Your Work.

This one is critical. Projects sometimes have a life of their own. Research can go on and on and the scope can expand and expand and expand. The limitations usually are dictated by the assignor's directive and the assignee's available time before the deadline. Given the breadth of possibilities, it is important to define the scope of the work done when presenting the outcome. For example, if you have been tasked with researching something, in presenting your research, state in advance the period your research spanned, the resources you used, and any avenues you were unable to cover. "I researched X only. I did not look at Y or Z." Defining your work in this way protects you in case different information would have been revealed through expanded research.

Tip No. 91

Be a Good Boss to Those You Oversee.

Be specific when assigning work and make sure everyone is clear on the directives. Remember, their mistakes are your mistakes. Position them to succeed and make sure they know your door is wide open for questions. Provide honest and thorough feedback and support them in growing to express their highest potential.

Tip No. 92

Give Credit Where It Is Due.

If someone else has done work that has led to a successful outcome, credit them with that work. First and foremost, do it because it is the honorable thing to do. Taking credit for another's work is an unforgivable breach of trust, and if you are discovered, it will damage your relationship with anyone who finds out about it. Second, if someone else did the work, you have no idea whether the work is reliable, even if it has led to momentary success. If you claim credit for the work, you also will receive the blame for any flaws in the work.

Tip No. 93

Do Not Be Thin-Skinned.

You will have experiences on the job that are subjectively offensive. Wherever people of diverse purposes, personalities, and backgrounds assemble, someone's toes are bound to be stepped on. Someday, those toes may be yours. Lick your wounds and move forward. Make a clear-eyed decision on what should happen next. Was the offense intentional? Was it spoken out of anger? Was it said to throw you off your game and bait you into making a disproportionate response? Center yourself. Though an offense may feel disrespectful, it is not always intended to be. You want to moderate your emotions and ensure that any response you offer comes from a thinking space, not a reactive space. Finally, know that not everything requires a response from you. Some things are not worth dignifying, even under the guise of educating the other person. Let barking dogs bark. You have enough biting dogs to deal with!

Tip No. 94

Do Not Make Rushed Judgments.

If you do not have the information you need, try to get that information before you act. Rumor and word-of-mouth should not be a substitute for fact. Do your best to get the most concrete form of information available. When emotions are high, important decisions get botched. On the job, try to make clear-eyed judgments instead of rushed, uninformed, or emotional ones.

Tip No. 95

Make Your *"Yes"* Mean *"Yes,"* and Your *"No"* Mean *"No."*

Be reliable. Author of *The Four Agreements*, Don Miguel Ruiz, in his first agreement advises, be impeccable with your word. Impeccability means more than mere follow-through because it also includes discipline with the spoken word. Do not say things you do not mean. Do not say things that are not true. Do not speak loosely. Speak consciously. Only say what you mean. Only say what you are willing to be a stand for. When you have said it, stand for it. That is how you get a reputation of reliability that others will stand behind too.

Tip No. 96

Offer Support.

When you see your colleagues struggling at work or in their personal lives offer to support them. It does not matter where they are positioned in the hierarchy. Everyone needs support from time to time. Whether or not the offer is accepted, it certainly will be appreciated. This is not about one-upmanship or being patronizing. It is about being vulnerable. And, to be effective, it may require you to be transparent. For example, "I know how challenging things can get sometimes." (Though, it does not include bringing your personal problems into the office. So, for example, do not offer this: "I have problems with my marriage too.") No one wants someone to stand above them and reach down with a hand. Stand beside them with an awareness of your weaknesses, and from that position, offer support. This is the right thing to do. It also strengthens your network and reminds you to ask for an assist when you need one.

Tip No. 97

Show Much Appreciation!

You can never be too thankful. A good "thank you" is its own form of payment. When someone on the job helps you out, make a big deal about it, even if helping you out is their job. Lots of people do terrible work on their job. If someone has done good work, that work is to be celebrated. Sing their praises! Tell them how much you value them. It costs you nothing and makes the other person feel great. Besides, when your co-workers see how effusive you can be, they too will want to be on the receiving end of your praises, and you may just find yourself surrounded by helping hands.

Tip No. 98

Pick Your Battles Carefully.

Sometimes, a fight cannot be avoided, but you must pick your battles carefully. Here are a few questions you can ask yourself when deciding whether the battle is worth fighting. First, is it winnable? Second, can someone else fight it for you or is this a battle you must fight for yourself? Third, will you sustain lasting damage, even if you win? Fourth, is that damage something from which you can recover? When you have addressed these questions, if you still think the fight is necessary, do an emotional inventory and discover what emotions are fueling you. Finally, develop a solid plan to recover from any blowback the fight may cause.

Tip No. 99

Befriend Lame Ducks.

When people are set to leave the company, either through termination or resignation, many of their colleagues abandon them. Perhaps their colleagues believe termination to be contagious or that the job will view maintaining a relationship with a departed colleague as disloyal. These beliefs are shortsighted. By adopting a different position, you can stand out. Reach out to your colleague and you will earn their respect. Your compassion will be remembered. This is one of those moments where it is more important to be loyal to your career than to your job. Of course, do not criticize your job with the lame-duck or provide the lame-duck with information the job would not want you to share. You are not reaching out to the person to share some sense of dissatisfaction with the job; you are reaching out to maintain a relationship you have built with a person you have been working with. Lame ducks land! Your network will be strengthened if you place value in the people you work with, not just the institutions.

Tip No. 100

Never Rest on Your Laurels.

Never stop doing your best. Never stop innovating, learning, and growing. Never fool yourself into believing you have finally "made it." No matter what level you have reached, keep working to advance your career.

Remember, in most circumstances you are only as valuable as your last accomplishment. Do not rely on your past achievements or accolades to justify your continuing value to the company. Employers have short memories. Most jobs are about, "what have you done for me lately!" Also, continuing to engage at the highest level will maintain your confidence and enthusiasm, and assure your ability to make a transition to another employer if desired or required.

Tip No. 101

Do Not Rely on Promises. Be Your Own Leverage.

On a job, as in life, promises are made and broken every day. Do not rely on promises. Make yourself valuable! Be excellent and be emotionally and socially competent. When you are valuable, you can leverage the organization's desire to keep you to get the things you need and want.

If you are told to wait or promised a future good, that is a present, "no" that may never become a "yes," notwithstanding promises made. The most certain way to transform a present "no" into a future "yes" is to increase your value to the organization. Even becoming more valuable may not work if the reason the organization said "no" had nothing to do with your importance. If the organization wanted to say, "yes" but for fiscal or other reasons could not, increasing your value may not help. Do not be afraid to leave and develop a plan to do so if your needs are not met. You are valuable and you deserve to be treated accordingly!

Choose Integrity, Alignment, and Joy. Nothing Plastic Is a Substitute for Divine Connection!

Conclusion

*You can make a difference. You can change
the world. Because you are the world.*

~ Federico Peña ~

*Each individual's willingness to take action to
sustain his or her own energy produces a powerful
influence that has the potential to affect healing
throughout the community and even the world.*

~ Roger Jahnke ~

*Do not inflict your will. Just give your love. The soul will
take that love and put it where it can best be used.*

~ Emmanuel ~

(Channeled information by Pat Rodegast)

*If you could get up the courage to begin,
you have the courage to succeed.*

~ David Viscott ~

Go forward and be "Godfulldent": confident in, and full of, God! Remember life on the physical plane is temporary. Do not expect your job to be permanent; even the best job is temporary. Be intentional! Choose purpose over permanence, position, and power. You are on the job to be an agent of holy transformation, work fearlessly!

> *Everything begins and ends with consciousness!*

This is a book of information and activations. It is only as valuable as your will to use it! I ask that you appreciate the information (increase its value) by engaging the activations. Do the work. There is no substitute!

Once you have gone as far as you can go alone, get external support. Team up with another, an accountability partner, or a coach, to turbocharge your growth.

In this final chapter, we discuss the consciousness that underlies everything offered in this book. Everything begins and ends with consciousness!

Our journey is full of awe and wonder, so many levels to awakening, some beautiful, some uncomfortable, all necessary! As we experience it all, we are to deliver our Divine Self, our authenticity, our best. Who is our best? What our Divine Self looks like is a unique and mysterious unknown. If I had to generalize what we are growing toward, I would say it approximates what Saint Francis of Assisi asked of the Lord in the beautiful Peace Prayer.

Peace Prayer

Lord, make me an instrument of Your peace.
Where there is hatred, let me sow love;
Where there is injury, pardon;
Where there is doubt, faith;
Where there is darkness, light;
Where there is sadness, joy.
O Divine Master, grant that I may not
so much seek to be consoled as to console;
to be understood as to understand;
to be loved as to love
For it is in giving that we receive,
It is in pardoning that we are pardoned, and
it is in dying that we are born to eternal life.

Reverend Kelli: I love that prayer! Immersing myself in beauty, like the beauty of this prayer keeps my energy balanced and acts as a buffer that repels triggering energies.

Sensei Subira: Yes! Reverend Kelli, thank you so much for involving me in this project. I predict that this book is going to change lives, and I feel fortunate to have been a part of it.

Reverend Kelli: Thank you so much, Sensei Subira! Your support has been invaluable.

Sensei Subira: Now, there is something I have been thinking about. The chapter with the coaching tips seems like it will be incredibly helpful to people. By itself, it may make such a difference in a person's work life. I feel like some people may choose to follow those tips only, especially people who are intimidated by fear of losing their job. What encouragement can you offer to support people in overcoming fear and choosing to embody their Divine Self?

> *No matter how great you are at your job or how great you are in general, you can be sabotaged by a system of thinking that takes hold of you and makes you feel that your choices are limited.*

Reverend Kelli: Some hide their Divine Self because they are afraid of the consequences of revealing who they truly are. Jobs can be intimidating. Some workplaces can seem very dark.

Former First Lady Michelle Obama, in her book *Becoming,* tells of feeling empty, when she worked as an attorney. She speaks generally about the fatigue, stress, and unhappiness among attorneys. She describes telling herself that the work was important and that she had no choice. She describes the feeling of only being as good as the hours billed and speaks of what she calls "the corporate ant mound." She speaks of her blinding drive to excel and her need to do things perfectly. She bemoans not thinking through her passions or how they might align with work she would find meaningful, what she describes as a more virtuous job. She outlines what I will call *silent internal pressure,* born of her awareness of her father's pride in her accomplishments and her belief that her mother would see her desire for fulfillment as a "rich person's conceit." She felt all of this angst over a job she was good at, and I would guess, in no danger of losing.

Sensei Subira: I am going to agree with you there. I doubt anyone would fire Michelle Obama, even before she became First Lady!

Reverend Kelli: Exactly! Yet as competent and confident and qualified as she was, look at all the thoughts that roiled within her. My point is, no matter how great you are at your job or how great you are in general, you can be sabotaged by a system of thinking that takes hold of you and makes you feel that your choices are limited.

The job is just the out-picturing of the shared consciousness of the people connected to it. Like a person, a job can evolve to its purest potential.

But the Presence of the Lord is here and now, and where God is, there is freedom! You simply must ascend to experience it. Benjamin Franklin said: "Liberty will not descend to a people. A people must raise themselves to liberty. It is a blessing which must be earned." When you experience doubt, fear, or resistance, you must greet it and treat it. You treat it by doing the work.

Let us return to the First Lady for a moment. She is an on-the-job champion! Regardless of her misgivings, no one can doubt that she was on the right job at the right time. She evolved beyond at least one unwritten but commonly understood rule that dictates that you not date those you work with. She ascended to a place of freedom. And, together, she and her husband, President Barack Obama, changed America and the world. Michelle Obama rose to fulfill her Divine Destiny.

The job is in your life to act as a spiritual training ground. You have to surrender and allow that to happen. If you are hiding or cowering, you cannot maximize the training opportunity or be a full resource for others and the job itself.

Sensei Subira: For the job itself?

Reverend Kelli: Yes, the job is just the out-picturing of the shared consciousness of the people connected to it. Like a person, a job can evolve to its purest potential.

Think about the sacred tradition of work and community. Work was a way people survived together. It was not a separate thing. Work and community were the same. Work was a sacred engagement.

The consciousness you take to the job has a real influence. Wrong is produced incrementally, like a slow-cooked frog, one unchallenged corrupt idea at a time. Your

Whatever workplace you find yourself in, God has positioned you exactly where you are.

consciousness can be the thing that steers the ship a degree to the right and allows it to miss the iceberg. Corporations and other jobs are worthy of an opportunity to remember their own Divine Identity and sacred purpose. If God has positioned you to be the message bearer, the consciousness bearer, the oracle, you cannot turn your back on that responsibility. In the Bible, God directed Jonah to deliver a prophecy to the people of Nineveh, but because Jonah judged the people of Nineveh as dangerous and unworthy of salvation he fled by ship in the opposite direction. That decision did not go well for Jonah. He was tossed overboard in a storm and saved from drowning by a big fish, spent three days in the fish's belly, and was only released when he repented. And where was he released? The shores of Nineveh!

Sensei Subira: So, we are doing our spiritual practice on the job, not only for ourselves but also to benefit the job spiritually?

Reverend Kelli: Yes, it is a sacred reciprocal relationship. I am here to say, whatever workplace you find yourself in, God has positioned you exactly where you are.

You are perfect for what is required, whatever that is! And, it is perfect for you, for now! Connect with God. Exploit the fact that you have Divine backing and do what God has placed you there to do. Be who God created you to be. Let God manifest Itself as you. And be your Divinity out loud, not quietly, but boldly!

Sensei Subira: But, Reverend Kelli, what if the job is like the pharaoh in the story of Moses whose heart was hardened and repeatedly rebelled against God's directive? How do we get the job to evolve?

> *You are God's seed. Be willing to plant yourself.*

Reverend Kelli: Well, Sensei, as you know, in that story, the Jewish slaves did eventually go free. Divinity, once unleashed, is irresistible. It never fails us, but our persistence sometimes does. We must be like the old widow Jesus spoke of in Luke 18:1-8, whose fearless, relentless persistence gained the favor of an unrighteous judge, a judge who neither feared God nor regarded man. Fearlessness and relentless persistence never fail to carry the day.

In the Bible, Jesus tells his disciples before sending them out: *What I tell you in the dark, speak in the daylight; what is whispered in your ear, proclaim from the roofs. . .. Are not two sparrows sold for a penny? Yet not one of them will fall to the ground outside your Father's care. And even the hairs of your head are all numbered. So, do not be afraid; you are worth more than many sparrows* (Matthew 10:27 & 28-31).

We are valuable to God. We must not hide our light under a bushel. You are God's seed. Be willing to plant yourself.

I once heard Reverend Dr. Michael Beckwith, founder of the Agape International Spiritual Center, tell a story about seed in a pocket. The story said that when you have a seed inside of a pocket, no matter how long it is in the pocket if it ends up falling out of that pocket into the right conditions, the right water, the right light, the right soil, it will grow. It will grow without complaint or regret over the past, no matter how bad that past was, no matter how dirty the pocket was, or how beat up the seed was in the pocket. The seed will still do what seeds do: it will grow!

This book has given you the information to create the right conditions. Now grow! Get started now and do what you can. Focus on what you can do, not what you are unwilling or afraid to do. Get started! Whether you have a job that you love, a job you hate or have no job at all, you have Divine work to do. It is yours to do in every moment. So, do not hold back, do not delay! Get to it! That is my advice. Get to it! And, one last thing, Sensei.

Sensei Subira: What is that Reverend Kelli?

Reverend Kelli: I want to offer a couple of warnings and a final offering.

First, spiritual practice is a path of growth. You will still occasionally do things you are not proud of. Do not believe yourself to be above mistakes.

When you think yourself too "good" a person to have done what you did, you will squirm, and worm, scream and blame, turning yourself inside out to avoid accountability. But, accountability is where the growth is! Embrace the facts. Facts do not make you good or bad; they are only information you can process and use to expand your self-understanding, self-acceptance, and self-love. These three are pillars of growth.

> *Love God not as myth but as manifestation.*

Second, the tools and practices offered here are powerful. But do not get cocky. The people you work with also are God's people. You are entrusted with them to love and care for them, not to take advantage of them or treat them as playthings. If you misuse what you have learned or use it in ways that are harmful to others, if you curse others instead of blessing them, you will position yourself for self-correction. In other words, God in you will bring you back into alignment by acting to correct you, and that action may not be pleasant. These tools are to help you, to advance you, to advance others, and to advance your workplace; they are not to be used to hurt anyone.

Finally, holy men and women, know that it is not being on the mountain that keeps the holy, holy. Those who are holy take the mountain with them by raising the energy wherever they are. It is not only the tools and principles that matter, but also the consciousness from which the tools and principles are applied. Apply them from a consciousness of alignment and amplification. Align with God and amplify the influence of that which you are in God, revealing more of the God that lives in you, shedding more of that which is false. Love the Lord your God with all your heart, mind, and soul, and love your neighbor as yourself. Love God not as myth but as manifestation.

God is not the myth you have made up in your mind or the myth you have been taught about. God is in front of you, behind you, and within you. God manifests in you and in me and in the events of our life. Love that God!

This book has supported you in priming yourself, in creating triggers that will take you back to your connectedness with God, to remind you to be grateful to God, to remind you to love God. Every tool is just a trigger, taking you back to the two main commandments: love yourself and others as the manifestations of God that you are, and love God.

The universe we have on the job and at home is the one that the vehicle of our communal consciousness has ushered into creation, as it co-creates with God. We cannot experience a better external world until we become a better world internally. That is the duty of each of us, wherever we find ourselves!

Sensei Subira: This has been an amazing journey! Reverend Kelli, how can folks find you if they want more information, and what kinds of services or programs do you offer?

Reverend Kelli: Well, as you can see, I love to talk! I am available for speaking engagements and, of course, I continue to offer private coaching. I also have created half-day, full-day, and weekend workshops on this topic. To keep up with what is happening, like our Facebook page https://bit.ly/3hyuW6d.

I also offer specialized coaching and workshops on Anti-Racism and diversity, and the minority and LGBTQIA+ experience at work.

I offer spiritual mediation services through which I am available to mediate disputes applying my mediation process based on practices similar to those outlined in this book. That work is available to businesses and employees, families, and individuals.

Finally, I invite folks to connect with our church, the GROW Continuum. Check us out on Facebook where we have a group https://bit.ly/32CGnpr and a page https://bit.ly/3moSKwZ. Like my Facebook page https://bit.ly/32CAxo2 and friend me https://bit.ly/32xVhgt.

Do It Now! Be Bold! Be Consistent! Reach Out!

Index

A
Acceptance 87, 88
Agency theory 122
agentic state. 117, 119, 121
alignment 1, 11, 16, 23, 36, 42, 47, 54, 55, 56, 57, 61, 62, 64, 87, 103, 110, 135, 158, 159, 164, 285
altar 85, 93, 146
Asch Paradigm 119
authority 5, 6, 7, 16, 52, 117, 118, 121, 123, 125, 174, 227

B
blessing 36, 37, 51, 57, 64, 94, 96, 110, 139, 142, 282, 285
Breathe and Bless 64

C
coaching iii, 16, 19, 20, 30, 47, 84, 97, 133, 149, 150, 151, 152, 153, 180, 203, 281, 286
company man 116
company woman 116
conform 16, 111, 116, 118, 178
connected thinking 115
Connection Portal 78, 79, 80, 81, 86, 88
continuum of genius 26, 27, 42, 48, 52
courage 88, 279
craft above calling 163
Creativity 87, 88, 262

D
Deep breathing 86
denials 54, 56
detachment 60, 65
disengaged engagement 62
Divine energy 41
Divine Identity 1, 5, 6, 11, 24, 114, 126, 127, 147, 148, 152, 283
Divine Self i, vi, 1, 3, 5, 8, 9, 10, 11, 12, 16, 17, 25, 28, 32, 36, 50, 51, 52, 53, 54, 55, 56, 60, 70, 73, 78, 82, 102, 111, 130, 133, 162, 166, 280, 281
Doublemindedness 110
droning process 117

E
EDI 52
EDMAM 95, 96

Emotional Freedom Technique 83
energy 2, 5, 6, 18, 25, 28, 29, 34, 35, 37, 51, 52, 53, 54, 57, 63, 65, 68, 70, 72, 73, 74, 83, 85, 86, 87, 88, 89, 90, 92, 93, 94, 95, 96, 98, 99, 102, 103, 104, 105, 115, 116, 137, 138, 153, 154, 160, 171, 172, 184, 187, 197, 198, 231, 279, 281, 285, 291
entrained 121, 125
Establishing the Proofs 91
exercise 44, 115, 150, 171

F
faith 33, 36, 46, 63, 73, 83, 89, 91, 132, 144, 147, 150, 154, 280
foundation 45, 68, 89, 99, 119, 164
fruits of the Spirit 92, 93
Fueling the Prayer 93

G
groupthink 110, 111, 112, 114, 115, 116, 121, 125

H
heroic past 48
High Council 97
holy contagion 60
hybrid tool 97

I
implant 91, 94, 95, 96
imprint 98
inspiration 33, 41, 42, 87, 112, 113
intention 6, 10, 25, 79, 83, 86, 87, 98, 99, 138, 148, 258

J
Jesus 4, 6, 9, 39, 52, 64, 70, 83, 93, 110, 112, 113, 114, 152, 284

K
Karoshi 157, 160, 161, 162, 165, 166

L
legacy quest 43

M
magic formula 22
Mantra 68, 69, 71, 72
Master Tool 78, 79
Milgram 122, 123, 124, 292
miracles 7, 41, 42, 48, 113

P
Peace 59, 80, 86, 280
peer pressure 119, 120

permanence 23, 24, 43, 280
persistence 10, 284
prayer 2, 10, 11, 34, 69, 72, 80, 86, 88, 89, 91, 92, 93, 94, 95, 96, 146, 150, 151, 152, 281
proof statements 91
proximity 34, 35
Psalm 90
Purifying the Prayer 92
Purifying the vessel 93

Q
quit power 43, 44

R
raising the vibration 94
Reality Reversal 79
resistance 53, 54, 55, 56, 57, 72, 73, 74, 78, 80, 83, 84, 87, 88, 90, 95, 102, 145, 261, 282
running your racket 106

S
scriptural and meditation apps 86
Serenity Prayer 88, 89, 95, 292
smudging 6, 85, 86
Social Identity Theory 119
sound 64, 68, 71, 79, 86, 105
strength 12, 58, 161, 172, 185
success vi, 1, 2, 9, 11, 23, 36, 43, 50, 68, 83, 110, 133, 134, 137, 141, 151, 158, 169, 172, 184, 214, 215, 224, 239, 245, 251, 260, 269

T
True Boss 40
True Work vi, 2, 8, 9, 10, 11, 16, 17, 25, 27, 30, 34, 35, 39, 40, 41, 42, 43, 44, 47, 48, 50, 54, 55, 56, 63, 68, 71, 72, 98, 130, 133, 143, 148, 154, 155, 166

W
white light covering 99
Wisdom 12, 89

Endnotes

1. The interview portions of this book are not verbatim accounts of the live interview; much of the material presented in interview format was not included in the interview and has been crafted to facilitate the delivery of the information in the book.
2. "The Power of a Name: The Power of Naming" by Rabbi Andrew Davids is an excellent article on this issue, which can be found at https://bit.ly/35N74d3.
3. I find it useful to read Scripture in many versions to get the nuance and all the different shades of meaning that others have attributed to the text. In this book, I sometimes quote all or part of a Scripture to make a point. I encourage readers to reflect on the entire Scripture in context using whatever version of the Scripture they prefer, so I do not identify the specific translation used for each citation. The Bible has been translated and reinterpreted many times, and I find it helpful to look at many different interpretations. The King James Version is a standard and I often use it here. The New International Version also is a version I use often. The Message Bible offers unique and understandable interpretations, as does the Weymouth New Testament, cited in this instance, and available online here: https://bit.ly/2FKxnFr.
4. I encourage you to learn more about Sensei Subira by connecting with her through her Facebook page: https://bit.ly/3iCb1Vr. Sensei Subira designed the process that resulted in this book. For medical reasons, she was unable to conduct the interview, but it was agreed that her name would be used and that the team member who substituted as interviewer could remain anonymous.
5. IVISD is the Inner Visions Institute of Spiritual Development, founded by Reverend Doctor Iyanla Vanzant; for more information, visit https://www.innervisionsworldwide.com/. Unity Village is a village in Jackson County, Missouri, and is the home of Unity Worldwide Spiritual Institute and the headquarters of Unity Worldwide Ministries. For more information, visit https://www.unity.org/.
6. Brother Ishmael Tetteh is founder of the Etherean Mission, Accra, Ghana, West Africa; for more information on Brother Ishmael Tetteh, visit https://ethereanlife.com/.
7. Defining consciousness is its own study and is beyond the scope of this book. For purposes of simplicity when used in this book "consciousness" refers to an ethereal energy of being emanated from one's thoughts, beliefs, emotions, experiences, genetics, and soul imprints that has the power to impact one's experience of reality.
8. https://bit.ly/3hz6QIl
9. Initiates, Three. The Kybalion: A Study of the Hermetic Philosophy of Ancient Egypt and Greece, by Three Initiates. Franklin Classics Trade Press, 2018.

10 DR. BRONNER'S LAVENDER ORGANIC HAND SANITIZER, https://www.drbronner.com/, 1-844-937-2551.
11 The Serenity Prayer by Reinhold Niebuhr
12 Disney's Academy Award winning 1958 documentary, White Wilderness, depicts what appeared to be the mass suicide of hundreds of lemmings. However, the scenes in the movie depicting lemming suicide were staged.
13 Much of the content concerning social science experiments on conformity and the agentic state is derived from publicly available research articles; most significantly, Haslam SA, Reicher SD (2012) "Contesting the 'Nature' of Conformity: What Milgram and Zimbardo's Studies Really Show." *PLoS Biol* 10(11): e1001426. https://bit.ly/32y82ru (including citations).
14 Code-switching is the practice of shifting the languages you use or the way you express yourself in your conversations.
15 The Psychology Dictionary
16 "More First Responders Dying by Suicide than in Line of Duty" by Courtny Gerrish, March 11, 2020, Spectrum News Wisconsin. https://bit.ly/3dShGZP.
17 National Institute of Mental Health https://bit.ly/3ohMSFN and Centers for Disease Control and Prevention WISQARS Leading Causes of Death Reports https://bit.ly/2ToIN6M.
18 National Vital Statistics Reports, Vol. 69 Number 11, September 11, 2020 by Sally M. Curtin M.A., "State Suicide Rates Among Adolescents and Young Adults Aged 10–24: United States, 2000–2018" https://bit.ly/3oq1kMX
19 **Instead of choosing suicide**, please call the toll-free National Suicide Prevention Lifeline at **1-800-273-TALK (8255)** or **text "hello"** to the crisis text line at **741741**. You can call or text 24 hours a day, 7 days a week. The service is free, confidential, and available to everyone who calls or texts. http://www.suicidepreventionlifeline.org. For information on suicide prevention visit: https://bit.ly/2Tjcmp2.
20 Baptist, Edward E. *The Half Has Never Been Told*. Basic Books, 2016.
21 National Museum of African American History and Culture, https://nmaahc.si.edu/.
22 "Wishing and Hoping," by Hal David and Burt Bacharach.
23 Versions of these questions can be found in Buddhist and Hindu teachings and Socrates also has been credited with having posed the questions.

Again, my memories are imperfect. I am sharing to the best of my knowledge and I have changed, identities, genders and circumstances as necessary to protect the privacy and the confidentiality of the people and matters involved. Similarities to actual people or events is unintended and for any such similarities I ask forgiveness.

www.ingramcontent.com/pod-product-compliance
Lightning Source LLC
Chambersburg PA
CBHW051039160426
43193CB00010B/994